To Gail,
with love from
Bruce

Chicago, 17 February 1978

VICTORIAN TASTE

Books by the same Author

GEORGIAN GRACE

VICTORIAN COMFORT

THE ENGLISH TRADITION IN DESIGN

MEN AND BUILDINGS

THE ENGLISHMAN'S CASTLE

GUIDE TO WESTERN ARCHITECTURE

A SHORT DICTIONARY OF FURNITURE

ENGLISH FURNITURE
(*The Library of English Art*)

TIME, TASTE AND FURNITURE

BRITISH FURNITURE MAKERS
(*Britain in Pictures*)

ARTIFEX, OR THE FUTURE OF CRAFTSMANSHIP
(*Today and Tomorrow Series*)

INDUSTRIAL ART EXPLAINED

THE MISSING TECHNICIAN IN INDUSTRIAL PRODUCTION

SELF-TRAINING FOR INDUSTRIAL DESIGNERS

HOW TO WRITE TECHNICAL BOOKS

A HISTORY OF CAST IRON IN ARCHITECTURE
(*In collaboration with Derek Bridgwater,* F.R.I.B.A.)

HOUSE OUT OF FACTORY
(*In collaboration with Grey Wornum,* F.R.I.B.A.)

HOME LIFE IN HISTORY
(*In collaboration with C. Thompson Walker*)

2000 YEARS OF ENGLAND

THE AMERICAN NATION
(*In collaboration with Julian Gloag*)

WORD WARFARE

WHAT ABOUT ENTERPRISE?

ADVERTISING IN MODERN LIFE

Mr. Gloag has also edited the following books:

DESIGN IN MODERN LIFE

DESIGN IN EVERYDAY LIFE AND THINGS

THE PLACE OF GLASS IN BUILDING

THE AGE OF REASON AND THE AGE OF FAITH

Above: The works of Sir Christopher Wren, shown in a single group, were exhibited as a "Tribute," by Charles Robert Cockerell at the Royal Academy in 1838. *Reproduced by courtesy of the Royal Institute of British Architects.*

Below: The frontispiece of Pugin's *An Apology for the Revival of Christian Architecture in England,* 1843, showing twenty-five of his works.

VICTORIAN TASTE

*Some Social Aspects of Architecture and
Industrial Design, from 1820–1900*

BY
JOHN GLOAG

ISBN 06-492437-8

Copyright © 1962 John Gloag
First published 1962
This reprint published 1972

This book is copyright under the Berne Convention. No portion may be reproduced by any process without written permission. Enquiries should be addressed to the author's literary agent, A.D. Peters & Co., 10 Buckingham Street, Adelphi, London. WC2 N6 BU

Published in the U.S.A. 1973 by:
HARPER & ROW PUBLISHERS, INC.
BARNES & NOBLE IMPORT DIVISION

Printed in Great Britain by
Redwood Press Limited, Trowbridge, Wiltshire

Dedicated to
ALISON ADBURGHAM

CONTENTS

The Character of Victorian Taste	XV

CHAPTER		PAGE
1.	The New Patronage and the Discarded Heritage	1
2.	Romantic Gothic	10
3.	Christian Gothic	19
4.	Loudon and Downing	39
5.	Ruskin and Morris	71
6.	The Classic Tradition and the Unrecognised Style	101
7.	Ornament and Design	136

Sources of References in the text	159
The Plates	167
Index, by Dora Ware	169

ILLUSTRATIONS IN THE TEXT

Chapter 1   Page
Initial letter T from *Our Iron Roads*   1
Decorative labels used by apothecaries and confectioners   2
Electric-telegraph instruments, 1851   3
Adjustable easy-chair, 1832   5
Easy-chair with degenerate classic ornament: the habit of lounging   7
Beehives shown at the Great Exhibition   8

Chapter 2
Initial letter D from *The Young Ladies' Treasure Book*   10
Portrait of Sir Walter Scott in decorative frame   12
Frontispiece to *The Pickwick Papers*, by Phiz   13
Sezincote House, near Moreton-in-the-Marsh   14
Strawberry Hill, Twickenham   15
Gothic interior decoration and furnishing caricatured by A. W. N. Pugin   17

Chapter 3
St. Paul's Church, Hammersmith, 1882, and the original Parish Church, 1631   18
Initial letter B from *Temples Ancient and Modern*, by William Bardwell (1837)   19
Tower of St. Michael, Huyton   21
Catholic town of 1440 contrasted with the same town in 1840   23
Chichester Cross   24
King's Cross, Battlebridge, and its demolition   25
The West Cheap Conduit, 1479   26
Chained pump, St. Anne's, Soho   27
Contrasted residences for the poor   28
St. Marie's Grange, near Salisbury   31
Christchurch, Herne Bay, 1841, and Pugin's attack on false, pretentious Gothic   33
The Victoria Tower, Houses of Parliament   37

Chapter 4
Double detached villa in Porchester Terrace, Bayswater   40
Loudon's experimental glass roofs, 1818   42
Glass dome at Bretton Hall, 1827   43
Design for iron elbow-chair by Robert Mallet   45
Three types of Public House   46
Service side of bar-room counter   47
Grecian and Old Scots villas   48
Five-roomed house and cottage   50
Loudon's Commercial Gothic   52
Pugin's comment on Commercial Gothic, and Loudon's suggestion for "Indian" Gothic   53
Loudon's designs for detached and double cottages   54–55
Woburn Railway Station and a half-timbered cottage   56
Old English and thatched cottages   57
Wooden house in the Swiss style; cottage in the German Swiss style; and gate lodge and stable in the Swiss style   58

x   ILLUSTRATIONS IN THE TEXT

	Page
Villa in the Swiss style	59
Designs for entrance lodges	60
Downing and the American Scene: suburban cottage and ornamental farmhouse	63
Old English cottage and cottage villa in the bracketed mode	64
Italian style bracketed villa and small cottage or gate lodge	65
Interior of bedroom in the Gothic style	66
Parlour in simple Gothic and interior in bracketed style	67
Downing's house near Newburgh, New York	69

Chapter 5

Interior of All Saints, Margaret Street, by William Butterfield	70
Interior of St. James-the-Less, Westminster, by George Edmund Street	73
St. Giles's, Camberwell, one of Sir George Gilbert Scott's first churches	74
St. Mary's, Wimbledon, by Sir G. G. Scott and W. B. Moffatt	75
St. Mary Abbots, Kensington, by Sir G. G. Scott	76
St. Matthias, Richmond Hill, Surrey, by Sir G. G. Scott	77
Detail of arches, St. Pancras Station; and the old Fire Station, Richmond, Surrey	80
The front of St. Pancras Station and Hotel	81
The Royal Victoria Patriotic School, Wandsworth Common, by Rhode Hawkins	82
Eaton Hall, Chester, after reconstruction by Alfred Waterhouse	83
The Law Courts in the Strand, by George Edmund Street	85
St. Mark's, Battersea Rise, by William White	86
St. Columba, Shoreditch, by James Brooks	87
Columbia Market, Hackney, by Henry Astley Darbishire	89
Pulpit, exemplifying professional "religious art"	91
Bookcase and writing table, by Norman Shaw, and east side development of Vardens Road, Battersea	92
Sideboard by Philip Webb	94
Chimneypiece and furniture shown at the International Exhibition, 1862	96
Cabinet in mediaeval style	99

Chapter 6

Chapter heading from *The Rocket, or The Story of the Stephensons, Father and Son,* 1880	101
The Coal Exchange, in Lower Thames Street, London	102
Osborne House, Isle of Wight, by Thomas Cubitt in collaboration with Prince Albert	103
St. Thomas's Hospital, Lambeth, by Henry Currey	104
The Albert Hall	105
Court of the Victoria and Albert Museum	106
The Huxley Building, Exhibition Road, South Kensington	107
Standpipe and chimney tower on Campden Hill, Kensington	108
Two designs for factory chimneys, by Sir Robert Rawlinson	109
Congleton Viaduct and Maidenhead Railway Bridge	110
Components of the Railway landscape	111
Typical railway embankment on the London and North Western line	112

ILLUSTRATIONS IN THE TEXT

	Page
Shugborough Park Tunnel mouth	113
Eastern Counties Railway Station, Cambridge, and Paddington Station	114
William Moseley's Crystal Way	115
First cast-iron bridge, spanning the Severn between Madeley and Broseley; and the cast-iron bridge over the Aire at Leeds	117
Chelsea Bridge, by Thomas Page	118–119
Albert Bridge, by Rowland Mason Ordish	120
Hammersmith Bridge, by Sir Joseph Bazalgette, and the original suspension bridge by William Tierney Clark	121
The railway bridge that crosses the Mersey from Runcorn to Widnes, by William Baker and Francis Stevenson	122
The Britannia Bridge over the Menai Strait, by Robert Stephenson	123
Design for a chain bridge to cross the Forth, published in 1818. Profile and general view of the Forth Bridge, by Baker and Fowler	124
The Tower Bridge	125
Ferry gangway structure, Prince's Landing Stage, Liverpool. Early prefabricated cast-iron lock house, Tipton Green, Staffordshire	126
Cast-iron street furniture	127
Ornamental cast-iron dome, shown at the Great Exhibition	129
General view of the Crystal Palace in Hyde Park	130
South façade, showing principal entrance to the Crystal Palace, and interior view from South Entrance	131
Sir Charles Fox	132
Sir Joseph Paxton	133
Interior view of Smithfield Market, designed by Sir Horace Jones	134
Tailpiece, depicting George Stephenson, from *The Rocket, or the Story of the Stephensons, Father and Son*, 1880	135

Chapter 7

Natural ornament, distorted	138
Stork candelabrum, and ornamental fire dogs	139
Table and bookcase by G. J. Morant	140
Ornamental silverware: bell, inkstand, tea, and coffee service	141
Knife, fork, and spoon by Lambert and Rawlings	142
Silver wine flagons and claret jug	143
Sopwith's Monocleid Cabinet	144
Two ornamental clocks	145
Gothic clock	146
Two mantelpiece clocks	147
Examples of "Gothic" metalwork	148
Gothic-pattern wallpaper	149
Window in coloured glass, by Luke Limner	150
Decay of design in chair-backs	151
Designs for brackets, table ends, and chairs in cast- and wrought-iron	152
Garden seat and chair in cast-iron	153
Metal chairs with frames of flat metal strips	154–155
Association of classical and naturalistic motifs	156
Domestic iron and brasswork	157
Cast-iron balconet	158

LIST OF PLATES

The Age of Reason and the Age of Faith: C. R. Cockerell's composition of the works of Wren, and Pugin's drawing of twenty-five of his own works
Frontispiece

1. Interiors at Eaton Hall, Chester, after Buckler
2. Gothic in the Georgian Tradition: Fonthill Abbey; St. Luke's, Liverpool; Scott Memorial, Edinburgh
3. The Apotheosis of the Gothic Revival: Albert Memorials in Kensington Gardens and Manchester
4. John Ruskin and John Claudius Loudon
5. Robert Stephenson, A. W. N. Pugin, Sir George Gilbert Scott, and William Morris
6. Examples of Loudon's architectural work: Wood Hall Farm, Pinner, and double detached suburban villa in Porchester Terrace, Bayswater
7. St. Saviour's Vicarage, by William Butterfield; and The Red House, built by Philip Webb for William Morris
8. Paddington Station Hotel, by Philip Charles Hardwick; and the Garrick Club, by Frederick Marrable
9. The Langham Hotel, by John Giles; and New Scotland Yard, by Norman Shaw
10. The Natural History Museum, Cromwell Road, South Kensington, by Alfred Waterhouse
11. The Imperial Institute, by Thomas Edward Colcutt
12. Air view of the lay-out of South Kensington, from Kensington Gardens to Cromwell Road
13. The Greek Doric portico of Euston Station, and the portal of the Box Tunnel
14. General Railway Station, Chester, and Shoreditch Station, London
15. Interior of Temple Mead Great Western Railway Station, Bristol, by I. K. Brunel; and Lime Street Station, Liverpool, by William Baker and Francis Stevenson
16. Clifton Suspension Bridge, and Brooklyn Bridge, New York
17. Hungerford suspension bridge, and Saltash railway bridge
18. The Great Conservatory at Chatsworth, and Loudon's method of curvilinear glazing

LIST OF PLATES

19. The Palm House, Kew Gardens, Surrey, and the New York Crystal Palace
20. Interior decoration in the Coal Exchange, London, and base of cast-iron lamp standard, St. George's Hall, Liverpool
21. Decorative cast-iron work: balcony of house at Parkgate, Cheshire, and the gates of the Sailors' Home, Liverpool
22. Valance on platform roof of Battle Station, Sussex. Decoration in the Armoury at St. James's Palace, by William Morris
23. Throne in the House of Lords
24. The Victorian industrial scene. "A Street in the Valley," by Donald Matthews

REFERENCES

References to authorities, sources of quotations and so forth, are numbered consecutively, 1 to 141, and are set out under their appropriate chapters at the end of the book, beginning on page 159. Sources of illustrations and the names of artists are included in the captions, so are the references to any quotations relating to drawings or engravings.

THE CHARACTER OF VICTORIAN TASTE

WHEN we have outgrown the current nostalgia for the Victorian Age, we may come to regard it as a period of vigorous decadence, though endowed with virile generative powers that conceived and, after prolonged gestation, gave birth to the new Western architecture and industrial design of the twentieth century. That new architecture is perfectly acclimatised to "the wind of change" that is blowing through the whole world to-day; and Victorian architecture was just as happily adjusted to the confident solemnity and respectable standards of the great middle class suburban civilisation which arose and flourished in nineteenth-century Britain. There was a want of frankness about the purpose of design in Victorian buildings, furniture, and indeed nearly everything except the work of engineers, who created new forms without reference to prototypes, such as railway locomotives; though when they used new methods and materials for solving traditional problems, bridge building for example, they often imposed the external appearance of a traditional solution as though ashamed of their own innovations. The result was an architecture of hypocrisy which began in an atmosphere of playful, antiquarian fantasy in the eighteenth century, passed through its well-mannered, picturesque and romantic phases during the 1790's and the Regency, becoming commercialised in the 1820's, and finally gathering ponderous strength from the moral earnestness of the Gothic Revival. Victorian taste was oppressed and distorted by that revival, which gave a religious tone to architecture, as, a century later, progressive beliefs about the structure of society gave a political tone to the modern movement in design. Reactionaries detested the modern movement of the 1930's which, after the second world war, was recognised everywhere by intelligent and perceptive people as the characteristic architecture of the Western world; but the architecture produced by the Gothic revivalists was intrinsically reactionary; those who created it looked back, never forward, so in an age of fantastic material progress, architecture was out of step with science, engineering, commercial enterprise and industrial expansion.

Victorian taste was also confused by the belief that ornament and design were identical, and was profoundly influenced by a secret religion, to which men habitually and women occasionally gave not their souls but their bodies: the religion of comfort. That religion, or philosophy, of comfort was the subject of the previous volume in the three books I have written on the social history of design, from 1660 to 1900. Of these, *Georgian Grace* was the first,* *Victorian Comfort* the second,† and this book completes the trilogy. But despite all the eccentricities and variations of taste and fashion, a clearly recognisable English

---

* Published in 1956. London: A. & C. Black. New York: The Macmillan Company.
† Published in 1961. London: A. & C. Black. New York: The Macmillan Company.

tradition of design always struggles through, as insistent and emphatic as the English love of liberty, and declaring an attitude of mind that has, since pre-Norman times, characterised men who have worked in wood, stone, metal and other materials, and, in the second half of the twentieth century, has been inherited, perhaps unconsciously, by architects and industrial designers. In another book I have attempted to identify the persistent influence of this tradition, from the Middle Ages to the present day, for it has survived, and even during the shadows of the Victorian period emerged here and there as a bright, natural expression of native skill, irrepressibly vivacious by comparison with the anaemic falsities of mock Gothic and finical, drawing-board classic.*

The study of design in relation to life in any period has, until the present century, been a missing chapter in social history. The insufferably tedious doings of petulant or ineffectual politicians, statesmen, generals, and other professional great men, though variously recorded by biographers, skilled and unskilled, reveal little about the way most people enjoyed or endured life. Architecture reveals all. Controlling, inspiring or indirectly influencing the form and colour of environment, the architect and the designer are the infallible interpreters of the age they live in—infallible because they are unconscious of their powers of interpretation: those are incidental, unsuspected, and all the more potent for that reason.

* *The English Tradition in Design.* Originally published as a King Penguin book in 1947: new and enlarged edition issued by A. & C. Black, London, 1959. New York: The Macmillan Company.

CHAPTER I

THE NEW PATRONAGE AND THE DISCARDED HERITAGE

THE character of the Victorian period is illustrated by nearly everything that was made and used from the mid-1820's to the opening years of the present century, for the beliefs, ideas and taste of the age were foreshadowed over a decade before the Queen began her reign in 1837 and extended beyond her death in 1901, surviving among the elderly until the beginning of the 1914–18 War. Even if we ignored their literary achievements, with Scott, Dickens and Thackeray at the beginning and Kipling and Wells at the end, we should learn much about the Victorians from their architecture, the growth of their towns and cities, the casual disposition of industrial plant, and the contents of every type of home. From such evidence we could deduce turbulent enterprise, sincere piety, belief in scientific progress, reverence for respectability, and a possibly unconscious dislike of acknowledging material conveniences too openly. This dislike was disclosed by innumerable oddities in the shape and decoration of buildings and things of everyday use, so that their real form and function were often deliberately disguised, or entwined with ornament, like the initial letter on this page. Used originally for the opening chapter of *Our Iron Roads*, a mid-nineteenth-century work by Frederick S. Williams, this incongruous initial defeats the basic purpose of type, which is legibility. Apart from that, the use of sprays of holly and mistletoe, bay and rosemary with a rustic initial is strikingly inappropriate for a book about railways. The decline of standards in typography and lettering during the first half of the nineteenth century is shown on the next page by four specimens of labels, used by apothecaries and confectioners. The word functionalism had not been coined, but the Victorian designer would have rejected everything it stood for, and would have agreed with Michael Finsbury that "disguise is the spice of life."[1] The initial and labels are minor though not unsignificant examples of a persistent tendency to confuse design with disguise; but the

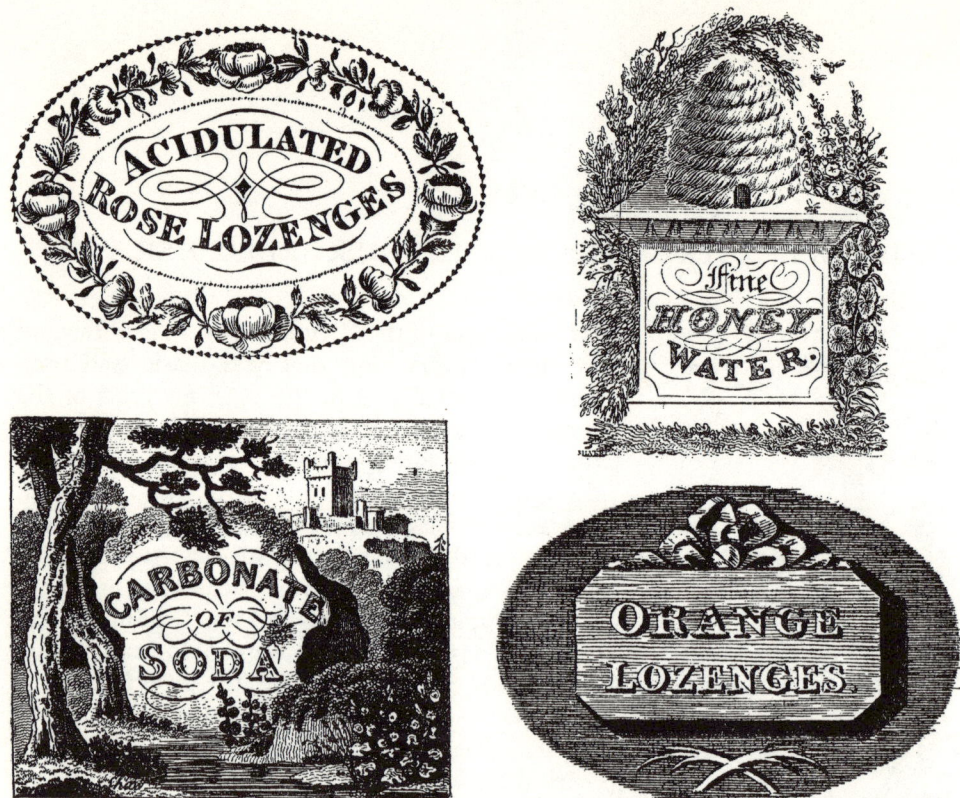

Decorative labels used by apothecaries and confectioners, of the kind pasted on bottles and packages during the first half of the nineteenth century. The classical tradition of the Georgian period survives in the lettering of Acidulated Rose Lozenges; there is a classical architectural note in the Honey Water label, though the lettering is degenerating in character and clarity. The Carbonate of Soda label reflects the spirit of the romantic movement, and the castle in the background could have taken an appropriate place among the scenes surrounding the portrait of Sir Walter Scott on page 12: the clumsy rendering of the word *carbonate* in sans serif capitals indicates the decline of respect for good Roman letter forms, and this is apparent too in the crudity of the lettering on the label for Orange Lozenges. *From the Author's collection.*

deliberate masking of scientific and mechanical appliances and engineering projects to hide their unfamiliarity of form was far more serious, because the practice delayed and distorted the development of industrial and architectural design. The results were often as peculiar as the electric-telegraph instruments, reproduced on page 3, which were invented, patented, and made by William Reid. They resembled memorial tablets, which gave users a choice of Gothic or classic frames, and showed how manufacturers were willing to oblige impartially the combatants on either side of the Battle of the Styles. Many of the great engineering achievements were partly hidden by a veneer of classic or Gothic detail, applied in the belief that an architectural need was thus fulfilled, without anybody suspecting that a new, authentic architecture was being suppressed. Even so, it was possible to detect the significance of the engineer as a designer, and one querulous critic, Samuel Sidney, after a severe attack on the massive Greek Doric gateway and internal planning of Euston Station, asked: "Why are our architects so inferior to our engineers?"[2] They had been one and the same person throughout the Graeco-Roman civilisation, the Middle Ages, and the early Renaissance, when men like Michelangelo and Leonardo da Vinci were architects, engineers, painters and sculptors. The separation of functions began during the seventeenth century when Jacques Lemercier was sent to report on a bridge near Rouen, accompanied by an "engineer." This was one of the first occasions when a distinction was made between engineering and architecture.[3] By the nineteenth century that former unity of art and science was forgotten: the engineer was a putter-up of structures, the architect a putter-on of styles. But no matter how they were disguised, the structures erected by engineers, and many of those designed by architects, exhibited all the robust vitality and exuberance of the Georgian and first Elizabethan periods, though they lacked the innate sense of style that distinguished both.

Electric-telegraph instruments, shown at the Great Exhibition, 1851, by William Reid, the inventor, patentee, and manufacturer. From *The Official Catalogue*, Class 10, item 427.

The appliances and articles that ministered to bodily comfort were seldom disguised. A richly furnished Victorian room was an upholsterer's paradise. The coiled spring for easy chairs and other seats came into use during the 1830's, and the first patent for this device in a mattress and other upholstery was granted in 1828 to Samuel Pratt of New Bond Street, London, a maker of camp equipment.[4] Within a few years, single and double cone spiral springs were being turned out in thousands by Birmingham factories, and their use altered the whole character of upholstered furniture.[5] The shapes of arm-chairs, sofas, settees and divans became softly corpulent and tended to relax elegance of posture in the home, though on formal occasions a decorous carriage was carefully preserved. A short book on manners, fashion and general deportment, which was published in 1842, denounced the easy-going tendencies of the times. "There is a practice getting into vogue," said the author, "almost into a sort of fashion, among young gentlemen who wish to impose upon the unwary, by *nonchalant* airs of affected ease and freedom from restraint, which I must here denounce as a breach of good manners, and a want of all just feelings of propriety;—I mean the practice of lounging in graceless attitudes on sofas and arm-chairs, even in the presence of ladies. All these vile and distorted postures must be reserved for the library-couch, or arm-chair, and should never be displayed in the society of gentlemen, and still less in that of ladies. In their own houses, ladies must submit to such conduct, as they cannot well leave a visitor to himself: at all other times they should, if they have any respect for their own dignity, give the lounger the cut-direct, and go to some other part of the room. Once denounced, however, as vulgar and uncivil, the nuisance will cease of itself; for the guilty only offend, under the impression of being thought superlatively fine."[6]

Dignity was valued by Georgian and Victorian society, though no Georgian man of breeding would have condescended to use either of the arm-chairs shown on pages 5 and 7: they would have outraged his sense of fitness and his feeling for style; he would have been horrified by the detail of their ornament and the invitation to boorish lounging conveyed by the line of their backs. Such ill-proportioned articles would not have been admitted to any gentleman's house before the early nineteenth century. But in a materialistic, commercial society, comfort was bound to win, for it was the permissible reward for all the strenuous progressiveness that made the Victorian age one of apparently irreconcilable contradictions: so revolutionary, so conventional, so materially successful, so morally earnest, so arrogantly confident in the present and future on earth, so pleased with the prospect of Heaven, so patronisingly contemptuous of the past, particularly the urbane Georgian past, so full of reverent admiration for mediaeval art and architecture.

Eighteenth-century historians like Gibbon could write about the society of Ancient Rome with easy and sympathetic familiarity, for Georgian and Roman artistic achievements were comparable, and classical architecture

THE NEW PATRONAGE AND THE DISCARDED HERITAGE

supplied a common environment for both; but many nineteenth-century historians and writers felt vastly superior to the ancient world. They had steam and all the power and the glory of mechanical achievement that went with it. Their world was committed to progress. They had little in common with the age of reason, although they were served and surrounded by devices that could not have come into use at all without the preparatory theorising and intellectual speculation which took place in that age and fertilised the inventive powers of some exceptional people, so that, in the words of H. A. L. Fisher, "A small handful of remarkable Scots and Englishmen, fewer than would be required for a football match, succeeded by their ingenuity in transforming the economic life of the country."[7] The Victorians were more distant in time from the Middle Ages than their Georgian forbears, but far closer in sympathy, for they regarded mediaeval England as a treasury of romantic riches and splendid architecture, though darkened by evil and cruel things, and the contrast between squalid barons in their insanitary castles, and well-washed, comfortably-housed members of the nineteenth-century middle classes kept the sense of superiority at a soothing temperature. An echo of Victorian faith in the inevitability of scientific progress was heard even after the first great war of our century had destroyed so many lingering Victorian convictions and prejudices, when J. B. S. Haldane in his essay *Daedalus, or Science and the Future* said, "Bad as our urban conditions often are,

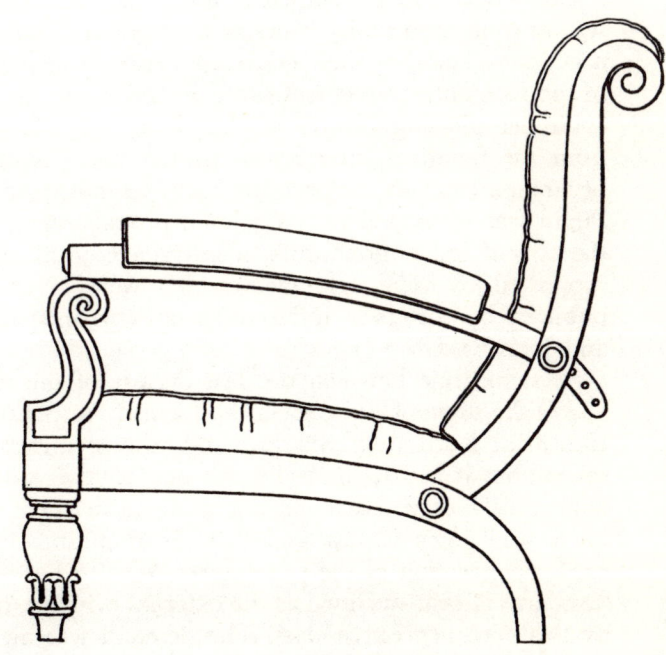

Easy chair with an inclined seat. In this design "the back may be lowered by removing the stud (which goes through the brass plates projecting at the back), and placing it in a lower hole, thereby suiting the inclination of the back to the fancy." From *The Modern Style of Cabinet Work*, plate 38. (London: T. King. Second edition, 1832.)

there is not a slum in the country which has a third of the infantile death-rate of the royal family in the middle ages."[8]

There were some awkward critics, like Pugin, who set out to deflate complacent materialism, but though his architectural erudition was respected, his savage book of *Contrasts*, first issued in 1836, was too powerful an irritant to be popular, for his illustrations and descriptions brutally disclosed what English towns and English life had lost since the early sixteenth century. Pugin achieved with graphic emphasis what Cobbett had attempted in his tedious tirade, *A History of the Protestant "Reformation," in England and Ireland*, published in 1824. Tennyson might refute such pessimism in verse that rang out as bravely as a trumpet call:

> ". . . Forward, forward let us range,
> Let the great world spin for ever down the
> ringing grooves of change."

But as a disillusioned old man Tennyson was converted to Pugin's point of view, when he wrote:

> "Yonder lies our young sea-village . . . Art and Grace are less and less:
> Science grows and Beauty dwindles . . . roofs of slated hideousness!"

Cobbett and Pugin helped to foster the legend of "Merrie England" which was to confuse so many issues in architecture and design for three-quarters of a century. Some of their contemporaries, who were enthusiastic participants in the Romantic movement that succeeded the age of reason and good design, could see glowing beauty in that imaginary, far-off land. Once dissociated from the fanatical intensity of purists like Cobbett and Pugin, the legend became artistically respectable and far more acceptable and popular, for Pugin was distrusted as a Catholic propagandist, and Cobbett had been, in the eyes of conventional folk, a subversive crank. But Pugin's indictment was supported by very ugly facts which were given increasing and consistent publicity by writers as different in outlook and character as Charles Dickens and John Ruskin.

At some time between the last decade of the eighteenth century and the 1840's the sense of civic, social and artistic responsibility was diminished. The Industrial Revolution was growing, almost unperceived at first, but like all revolutions it had its mob, for the new rich were on the march, all the more dangerously destructive for being silent in their unplanned capture of old towns and green valleys and their assumption of authority over a large and expanding section of the population. Wealth had outstripped education, and standards of taste declined as the external evidence of prosperity was demanded by this new, aggressive class. The demand was met, at first by slightly exag-

The coarsened remains of classical ornament appear in the cresting of the back; but that is the only trace of kinship with the Georgian age, which was only a couple of generations away. No Georgian gentleman would have allowed such a clumsy, ill-proportioned design in his house. From *The Modern Style of Cabinet Work*, plate 29. (1832.)

Left: No Georgian gentleman, even in his most relaxed moments, would have behaved like this Oxford undergraduate of the 1850's. From *The Adventures of Mr. Verdant Green*, by Edward Bradley (Cuthbert Bede), published 1853–56, page 132.

gerating what had been deemed correct by architects, tradesmen and craftsmen bred up in the classical Georgian tradition of design; but the new patrons of architecture and the ancillary arts soon became impatient of genteel restraints, and in the end they won the battle for ostentation. A philosophy of comfort, developed by the plutocracy and adopted by the middle classes, replaced educated taste, though this substitution was unperceived. There was plenty of "taste," but it was unregulated by critical standards and uninformed by any knowledge of what was well- or ill-proportioned. The heritage of good design was discarded, and the classical tradition that persisted far into the Victorian period lacked the imaginative virility of Georgian work, for the orders of architecture were no longer revered and used as a universal system of design, and the architect became a style-fancier instead of a master-designer.

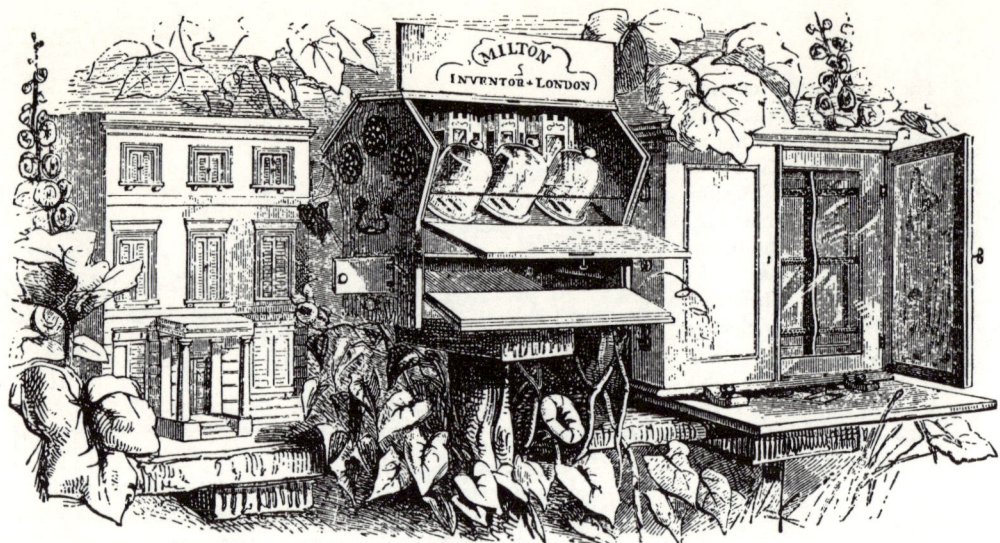

Three beehives produced by John Milton, of 10 Great Mary-le-bone Street, London, and shown at the Great Exhibition, 1851. *Left:* "The Town Mansion Hive." *Centre:* "The Royal Alfred Hive," described as "suitable for the conservatory, library, or any room where the sun's rays come during some portion of the day." *Right:* "The Unicomb or Mirror Hive . . . so constructed that the movements of every bee can be observed." From *The Official Catalogue*, Class 9, item 291.

The Battle of the Styles began, and continued with indecisive bitterness until neither routine classic nor revived Gothic bore much resemblance to their noble prototypes.

The classic orders of architecture had dominated every branch of design since the late seventeenth century; they were acclimatised late in England, having been regarded as Italianate intruders during the sixteenth century when they were grievously mishandled by joiners and carvers, masons and plasterers; nor was the true significance of their proportions and their capacity for resolving horizontal and vertical elements understood until the work of Inigo Jones and the writings of Sir Henry Wotton had supplied the examples and expounded the principles that enlightened both architects and their patrons. Inigo Jones did not live to see the golden age of good design which began after the restoration of Charles II and lasted until the 1830's, but Wotton's paraphrase of Vitruvius, which he published in 1624 and entitled *The Elements of Architecture*, was reprinted many times and described the classic orders with friendly familiarity, endowing them with human characteristics. To educated people, architecture meant classic architecture; as early as 1644, Evelyn, after a visit to Rome, described the Palazzo Farnese as "A magnificent square structure, of the three orders of columns after the ancient manner, and when architecture was but newly recovered from the Gothic barbarity." Gibbon expressed the belief of most Georgian gentlemen when he wrote: "The practice of architecture is directed by a few general and even mechanical rules."[9]

Gibbon was writing for an audience that was aware of those rules, for his contemporaries possessed a critical knowledge of classic architecture and an indulgent regard for the amusing variations of "the Gothic taste," which, like "the Chinese taste," were accommodated within the broad framework of the classic orders. In the middle years of the nineteenth century, Ruskin informed an Edinburgh audience that "Architecture is an art for all men to learn, because all are concerned with it; and it is so simple, that there is no excuse for not being acquainted with its primary rules, any more than for ignorance of grammar or of spelling, which are both of them far more difficult sciences. Far less trouble than is necessary to learn how to play chess, or whist, or goff, tolerably . . . far less than a schoolboy takes to win the meanest prize of the passing year, would acquaint you with all the main principles of the construction of a Gothic cathedral, and I believe you would hardly find the study less amusing."[10] The extent and character of Ruskin's influence are discussed in Chapter V; but his emphatic and uncompromising rejection of all the lucidity and orderliness of classic architecture should be quoted here. "Whatever has any connection with the five orders, or with any one of the orders," he wrote, "whatever is Doric or Ionic or Corinthian or Composite, or in any way Grecised or Romanised; whatever betrays the smallest respect for Vitruvian laws or conformity with Palladian work . . . that we are to endure no more."

It was the requiem of the age of reason.

CHAPTER II

ROMANTIC GOTHIC

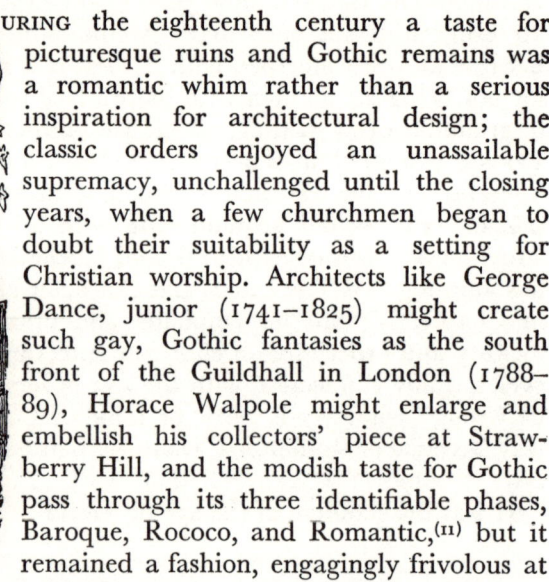

DURING the eighteenth century a taste for picturesque ruins and Gothic remains was a romantic whim rather than a serious inspiration for architectural design; the classic orders enjoyed an unassailable supremacy, unchallenged until the closing years, when a few churchmen began to doubt their suitability as a setting for Christian worship. Architects like George Dance, junior (1741–1825) might create such gay, Gothic fantasies as the south front of the Guildhall in London (1788–89), Horace Walpole might enlarge and embellish his collectors' piece at Strawberry Hill, and the modish taste for Gothic pass through its three identifiable phases, Baroque, Rococo, and Romantic,[11] but it remained a fashion, engagingly frivolous at times, always well-mannered, and blithely destitute of spiritual significance. Crumbling keeps and battlements, like those shown above on the decorative mid-Victorian initial, had been portrayed by innumerable artists and engravers from the time when Samuel and Nathaniel Buck began to publish their famous "views" of abbeys, deserted churches and ruined castles in the 1720's. Victorian artists took mediaeval ruins very seriously; Sir Walter Scott had peopled them with gallant knights, fair ladies, and monstrous barons; they stirred the imagination, so that the sinister Templar, Sir Brian de Bois-Gilbert, rode again, and Reginald Front-de-Bœuf, Cedric the Saxon, Isaac of York, the Prior of Jervaulx, Wamba the jester, and Wilfred of Ivanhoe came alive for the impressionable reader. For the Georgians, ruins were decorative and amusing, and even Walpole's Gothic story, the *Castle of Otranto*, though it gave impetus to the Romantic movement, did not encourage seriousness about the Gothic taste, though Walpole was serious enough about accuracy in copying mediaeval prototypes. When Batty Langley "endeavoured to adapt Gothic architecture to Roman measures" and "*invented* five orders for that style" he described him as a "barbarous architect." "All that his books achieved," he wrote, "has been to teach carpenters to massacre that venerable species, and to give occasion to those who know nothing of the matter, and who mistake his clumsy efforts for real imitations, to censure the productions of our ancestors. . . ."[12] But Batty Langley's works were popular, and the detailed directions he gave for the use of Gothic ornament on various internal and external features in such handbooks as *The Builder's Director or Bench-Mate*[13] had a large and receptive audience, for they were, as the author mentioned on the title page, "Written for the Use of *Gentlemen* delighting in True Architecture; and for *Masters* and *Workmen* to Draw from and Work after." Horace Walpole may have been repelled by such attempts to simplify the use of Gothic forms, but they had the effect of keeping the fashion orderly and its features symmetrical, until it became inextricably involved with the taste for the Picturesque. Sir Uvedale Price in his famous essay, *On the Picturesque* (1795), pointed out that symmetrical composition and picturesque effects were incompatible, for "among the various causes of the superior picturesqueness of ruins, compared with entire buildings, the destruction of symmetry is by no means the least powerful." His next sentence indicated the precise nature of the Gothic contribution to picturesque chaos. "In Gothic buildings," he wrote, "the outline of the summit presents such a variety of forms, of turrets and pinnacles, some open, some fretted and variously enriched, that even when there is an exact correspondence of parts, it is often disguised by an appearance of splendid confusion and irregularity." His use of the words "splendid confusion" indicates the Georgian attitude to Gothic architecture; it was an ephemeral fashion, associated with a fondness for ruins, genuine or contrived, nothing more. (See plate 2.)

Fonthill Abbey in Wiltshire, designed for William Beckford by James Wyatt and built between 1796 and 1799, was the most extravagant example of Georgian Gothic, with a tower, 276 feet high, and a hall, "built in the ancient baronial style, seventy-eight feet high, sixty-eight feet long, and twenty-eight feet wide." There was an oak roof, "decorated with sixty-eight shields, emblazoned with various family quarterings," and daylight was filtered through "three gothic windows of painted glass, on the right hand; the compartments of which are copied from some very ancient specimens in Canterbury cathedral."[14] John Rutter, describing the view towards the south-east, said that the Abbey formed "a grand mass of embattled towers, surmounted by the lofty octagon tower which composes the centre."[15] Fonthill was very obviously the caprice of a wealthy man of taste, like William Porden's original designs for Eaton Hall, Chester (1803–12), executed for Lord Grosvenor. (See plates 1 and 2.) The Romantic movement and the picturesque architecture through which it found such varied expression, adorned and sometimes

The impact of the Romantic movement on literature and architecture is symbolised in this portrait of Sir Walter Scott and the emblematical border. The portrait, from a miniature by Woolnoth, and the border, designed and etched by Hawksworth, form the frontispiece to *The Spirit of the Public Journals*, for 1825. The details of the arch are copied from the south entrance of Roslin Chapel, and "the escutcheons appended on either side, contain striking scenes from the Poet's most celebrated works. . . ." The vocabulary of those mediaeval romances contained words that were almost intoxicating to writers like Ruskin, who found a "strange and thrilling interest" in the sound of "Vault, Arch, Spire, Pinnacle, Battlement, Barbican, Porch, and myriads of such others, words everlastingly poetical and powerful whenever they occur. . . ." Words that sometimes deserved the label Robert Louis Stevenson invented—*tushery*. (See Scott Memorial on plate 2.)

disfigured the country with castellated structures, such as Luscombe, near Dawlish, Devonshire, 1800–4, by John Nash; Eastnor Castle, Herefordshire, 1808–15, by Sir Robert Smirke; Gwrych Castle, near Abergele, Denbighshire, completed in 1815, by Charles Augustus Busby, and Abbotsford, near Melrose, Roxburghshire, built for Sir Walter Scott in 1816 by Edward Blore and completed in 1822–23 by William Atkinson. Ruskin, who admired and often quoted the works of Scott, deplored his taste in architecture, and observed that while the author laid his scenes "in Melrose Abbey and Glasgow Cathedral, rather than in St. Paul's or St. Peter's, it did not enable him to see the difference between true Gothic at Glasgow and false Gothic at Abbotsford."(16)

When Abbotsford was built, Ruskin was unborn, Pugin only four years old, and no architect, no patron, not even Sir Walter Scott, recognised any moral obligations in their use of Gothic. It was an agreeable alternative to classic architecture, almost as orderly, unless architect and patron had taken Sir Uvedale Price too seriously and favoured a deliberately asymmetrical

Frontispiece to *The Pickwick Papers*, drawn by Phiz, the pseudonym of Hablôt Knight Browne (1815–82). This has a jovial Gothic border: there is nothing intense or romantic about its imps and hobgoblins: and although Mr. Pickwick and Sam Weller are sitting in a fearfully untidy room with a make-believe Gothic press in the background, it is obviously a cheerful and cosy room. Comfort was getting the upper hand of romance: but although the taste for comfort was growing it was, in Kipling's phrase, "Hedged in a backward-gazing world," so a typical English compromise was worked out: Gothic, Elizabethan, and Jacobean forms were muddled up together under the comforting label of "Old English," upholstery was improved, and the golden age of the antique dealer began. Many vivid passages in the works of Dickens glorify comfort, extol the pleasures of eating and drinking, and deride the humourless dignity that was a by-product of the Romantic movement.

composition: nor was it the only alternative. Thomas Hope had explored the works of countries that were ancient when the civilisation of Greece was still in its archaic phase, and Egyptian motifs competed with classical decoration in the early years of the nineteenth century,[17] so did Indian. Sezincote House, near Moreton-in-the-Marsh, Gloucestershire, was built in the Moorish style, in 1805, by Samuel Pepys Cockerell, for his brother, Sir Charles Cockerell (see page 14). William Porden used Saracenic ornament for the great rotunda and stables which he began to build in 1803 for the Prince of Wales to the north-east of the Pavilion at Brighton, apparently borrowing the details from prints of Agra and Delhi.[18] Porden's work there was supervised by his assistant, Peter Frederick Robinson (1776–1858), who became one of the commercially successful style-fanciers, always delighted to supply his clients with Old English designs—Tudor and Elizabethan half-timbered houses, or imitation Swiss chalets. He designed the Egyptian Hall in Piccadilly in 1811–12 (demolished 1904) and the Swiss Cottage at St. John's Wood, 1829–32.

Sezincote House, built in 1805, by Samuel Pepys Cockerell (1754–1827). From a drawing by J. P. Neale included in John Britton's historical and descriptive views of *Bath and Bristol with the Counties of Somerset and Gloucester*. (London: W. Evans and Co., 1829.)

Despite the antiquarian and exotic fancies of a few architects and their clients, Gothic remained as the chief alternative to classic, representing romance, with rather more popular emphasis as the sales of Scott's novels increased, but not threatening the established acceptance of the classic orders as the great system of design that could regulate the proportions of any architectural composition. Gothic for Romance: Classic for Reason: that was the civilised, tolerant Georgian view. The Victorians, less gracious but far more serious, would have none of it: Gothic for Christianity, Classic for Paganism, was the war-cry of the Gothic revivalists in the Battle of the Styles. We are still living with the results of that incoherent conflict, but before it became a moral as well as an aesthetic issue, the charming gentlemanly Gothic of the Georgian period was replaced by conscientious reproductions of the various phases of mediaeval church architecture, based on careful observation and study. Such copies and adaptations were lifeless, unlit by the faith that had inspired the original works, and lacking the modish air of make-believe of a Strawberry Hill or a Fonthill Abbey.

The first systematic study of Gothic architecture in England was made by Thomas Rickman (1776–1841), the son of a grocer and druggist, who began his career as an assistant in his father's shop, qualified and practised as a doctor, but gave up medicine after a couple of years and went into business, eventually becoming an architect. He was a self-taught draughtsman, an earnest student of church architecture, and the most important result of his studies took the form of a long article for Smith's *Panorama of Science and Art* (1812–15), which was reissued as a book in 1817 under the title of *An Attempt to Discriminate the Styles of Architecture in England, from the Conquest to the Reformation*.

This book ran into many editions, and ended a lot of confusion about English Gothic architecture by naming the different styles with such simplicity and lucidity, that Rickman's nomenclature—Norman, Early English, Decorated, and Perpendicular—was rapidly adopted and has been used ever since. "During the eighteenth century," he wrote, "various attempts, under the name of Gothic, have arisen in repairs and rebuilding ecclesiastical edifices, but these have been little more than making clustered columns and pointed windows, every real principle of English architecture being, by the builders, either unknown or totally neglected."[19] He believed that clear distinctions of style were "now almost entirely confined to churches; for the destruction and alteration of castellated buildings have been so great, from the changes in

Strawberry Hill, Twickenham, which Horace Walpole acquired in 1747 and transformed, so that it became the most famous example of fashionable Gothic. (*From a contemporary print in the author's possession.*) Such engaging frivolities were deplored by the earnest Gothic Revivalists. In his *Personal and Professional Recollections*, Sir George Gilbert Scott said: "It is almost vexatious when we consider how great an event that revival really has been, to recollect, at the same time, how unconscious one felt of this fact during its earlier years. I call these its earlier years, because I hardly view those which preceded 1830 (or even a later date), as belonging to the period of the revival at all. Writers on this subject are wont to talk about Strawberry Hill, and a number of such base efforts, as the early works of the revival. They may be so in a certain sense, but one can scarcely trace much connection between them and the work of its really vigorous period, and, as I personally know little, and knew nothing, about them, I will leave them wholly out of the question." (Chapter III, page 107.)

the modes of warfare, etc., that, in them, we can scarcely determine what is original and what addition."

Rickman built a large number of churches, many of them in the Perpendicular style, but although his details were immaculate, his approach to design was that of a Georgian architect.[20] He used iron for the internal structure of some of his churches, notably three he built in Liverpool with John Cragg, the ironmaster: St. George's, Everton, St. Michael's, Toxteth Road, and St. Philip's, Hardman Street.[21] The latter cost about £12,000, and was described in a contemporary guide book as a building in the Gothic style, with the external walls of painted brick and "the principal part of the work in the inside" and "the outside ornaments" of cast-iron.[22] Like John Nash, who used cast-iron for such classic features as the Doric columns of Carlton House Terrace and the colonnades of Regent Street, Rickman did not hesitate to reproduce Gothic tracery in this accommodating material. Perhaps he was, as Colvin suggests, "a better antiquary than architect."[23] His chief concern was accuracy, and he was unaware of any obligation to impart moral purpose to the structural methods or materials he employed. Because of his love of accuracy, he never allowed his work to acquire the flimsy air of the cheap commercial Gothic used by speculative builders, who took their designs from the innumerable copy-books that appeared in the 1820's and 30's, by architects like Peter Frederick Robinson, that prolific author of designs for every kind of building in every kind of style, and by John Claudius Loudon, the landscape gardener and architect, whose *Encyclopaedia of Cottage, Farm and Villa Architecture and Furniture* was issued in 1833, and became a best-seller. Such popular works supplied inferior material for imitation; they degraded Romantic Gothic, so that its former elegance and gaiety were forgotten.

The illustrations and specifications in Loudon's *Encyclopaedia* had an unfortunate and lasting influence upon the character of the Victorian scene, for they were concerned chiefly with the external trappings of various styles: Gothic, Greek, Italianate, Swiss, Indian, Old English, and Scottish baronial. The Christian Gothic Revival had nothing to do with such antics in brick and stone; the architects and writers who were engaged in spreading the belief that Gothic was the only architecture fit for Christians had little use for worldly fashions and the eccentricities of personal taste and no use at all for Romantic Gothic, or anything mellowed by Georgian graces. Their robust, earnest Gothic was the architectural counterpart of muscular Christianity. By turning their minds back to the mediaeval past they performed a profound disservice to the development of architectural design in their own day. In the words of Henry John Randall, "The Gothic Revival, especially in the nineteenth century, was one in which the perfection of the mechanism failed to conceal the departure of the spirit."[24]

Pugin drew this interior to illustrate "the extravagent style of Modern Gothic Furniture and Decoration," and included it as an awful warning in *The True Principles of Pointed or Christian Architecture* (1841). He observed that "upholsterers seem to think that nothing can be Gothic unless it is found in some church. Hence your modern man designs a sofa or occasional table from details culled out of Britton's Cathedrals, and all the ordinary articles of furniture, which require to be simple and convenient, are made not only very expensive but very uneasy. We find diminutive flying buttresses about an arm-chair; everything is crocketed with angular projections, innumerable mitres, sharp ornaments, and turreted extremities. A man who remains any length of time in a modern Gothic room, and escapes without being wounded by some of its minutiae, may consider himself extremely fortunate. There are often as many pinnacles and gables about a pier-glass frame as are to be found in an ordinary church, and not unfrequently the whole canopy of a tomb has been transferred for the purpose, as at Strawberry Hill. I have perpetrated many of these enormities in the furniture I designed some years ago for Windsor Castle." (Pages 40–41.) Compare this interior with those by Porden at Eaton Hall on plate 1.

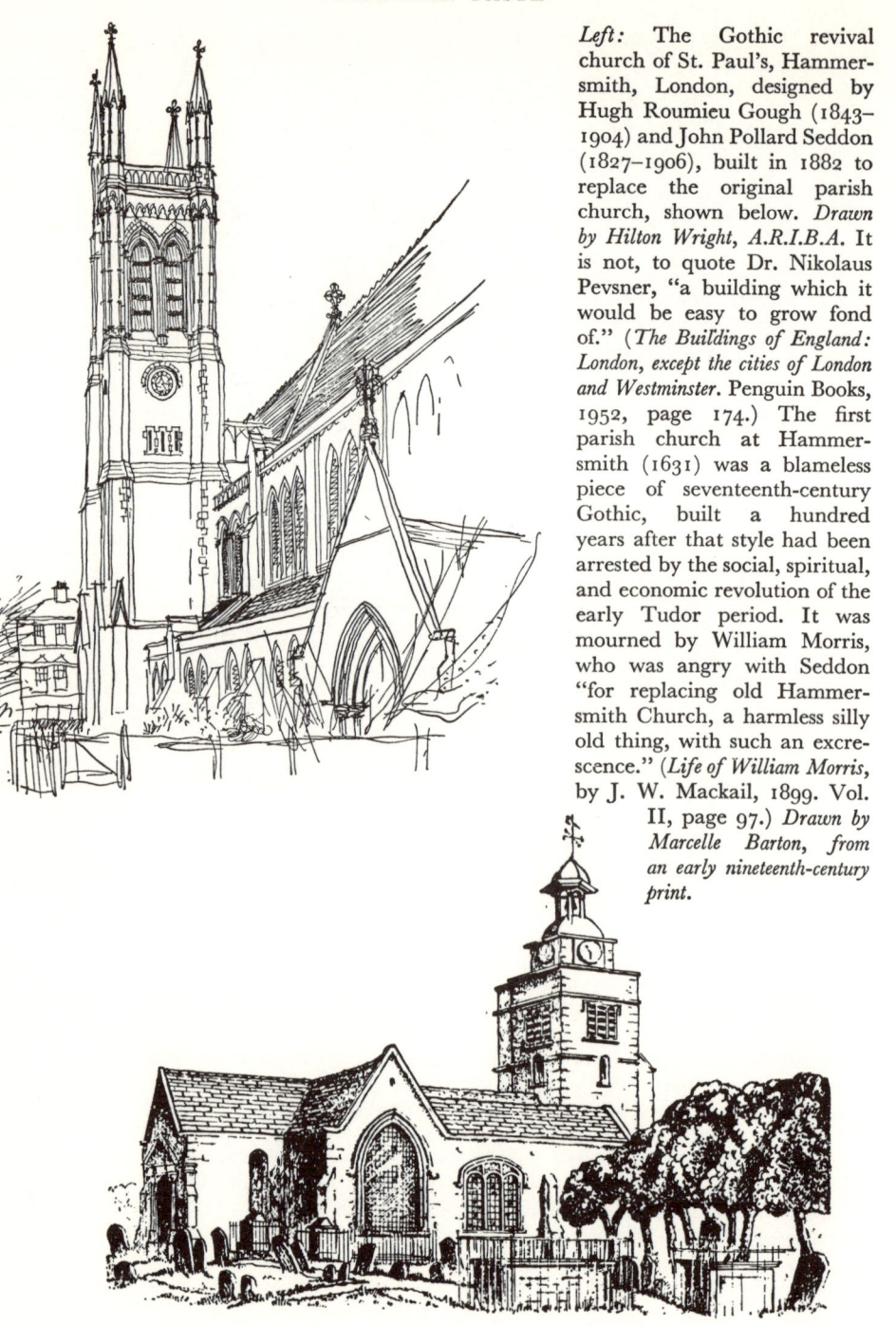

Left: The Gothic revival church of St. Paul's, Hammersmith, London, designed by Hugh Roumieu Gough (1843–1904) and John Pollard Seddon (1827–1906), built in 1882 to replace the original parish church, shown below. *Drawn by Hilton Wright, A.R.I.B.A.* It is not, to quote Dr. Nikolaus Pevsner, "a building which it would be easy to grow fond of." (*The Buildings of England: London, except the cities of London and Westminster.* Penguin Books, 1952, page 174.) The first parish church at Hammersmith (1631) was a blameless piece of seventeenth-century Gothic, built a hundred years after that style had been arrested by the social, spiritual, and economic revolution of the early Tudor period. It was mourned by William Morris, who was angry with Seddon "for replacing old Hammersmith Church, a harmless silly old thing, with such an excrescence." (*Life of William Morris*, by J. W. Mackail, 1899. Vol. II, page 97.) *Drawn by Marcelle Barton, from an early nineteenth-century print.*

CHAPTER III

CHRISTIAN GOTHIC

BECAUSE the word *revival* implied that forms long dead were being resurrected, the fact that Gothic architecture had never died out in England was ignored. But the native, pre-Renaissance style of building persisted throughout the sixteenth and seventeenth centuries, and survived in isolated areas until the present century, unconnected with any fashionable antiquarian studies by architects or their patrons. For instance, Hammersmith Parish Church was a simple Gothic structure, built in 1631, with a large east window, and a square tower crowned by a belfry; as unpretentious as any small country church of the previous two centuries.[25] It was demolished and replaced in 1882 by a Gothic revival church. (See opposite.) St. John's, Leeds, a large church built in 1632–33, was in the Perpendicular style; and a later church at Staunton Harold, Leicestershire, begun in 1653, was built throughout in that style which represented the last phase of English Gothic. When repairs and additions were made to existing country churches Gothic forms were generally used, not with any conscious or scholarly respect for historical proprieties, but because it was the natural thing for local builders to do. An example of this continuity of tradition in design is the tower of St. Michael, the parish church of Huyton, Lancashire, which has eight stone pinnacles surmounted by gilded metal wind-vanes in the form of pierced banners. The upper part of the tower was built after the Restoration, and has the date 1664 inscribed on the top. Over a hundred years earlier, in 1555, the church was a ruin, and repairs were carried out during the sixteenth and seventeenth centuries, but no attempt was made to introduce classical features. In the Cotswolds as late as the 1920's, small local builders, running a family business, often put into the houses they built early Tudor stone fire-places, not reproduced from measured drawings of some prized prototype, but naturally, for that was the way their fathers and grandfathers and great-grandfathers had built fire-places. Such work represented one of the unsevered threads of the English tradition in design, a tenuous connection between mediaeval civilisation and the twentieth century. A few pockets of such traditional skill existed throughout the Victorian age, but they were not susceptible to artificial expansion, even if anybody had thought of using them to create authentic Gothic buildings. They represented native Gothic, a little too humble and ordinary to be acceptable to the architects and propagandists who were reviving Christian Gothic with all the ardour of Crusaders determined to recapture the Holy Places.

The Christian Gothic revival drew some of its power from the Evangelical movement which had refocused all the old Puritan suspicion of art that gave pleasure, as opposed to art with a moral purpose, suspicion that was to be replaced by indifference after the educational work of Dr. Thomas Arnold began to take effect, and it was almost obligatory for an English gentleman to be a pious, hearty Philistine. By becoming associated with a religious movement, an emotional drive was put into an architectural style that gave its advocates and practitioners an irresistible sense of rectitude, and the most outstanding of these were two men of indisputable genius, Pugin and Ruskin.

Augustus Welby Northmore Pugin was born in 1812, and died at the early age of forty. He was the son of Augustus Charles de Pugin (1762–1832), a refugee from the French Revolution, who landed in Wales in 1791, penniless, hardly able to speak English, untrained for any kind of work, but possessing an amateurish facility for drawing. He found employment as a draughtsman in the office of John Nash, who was at that time practising in South Wales. Sir John Summerson in his biography of John Nash points out that at first Pugin could have been "little more than a learner, probably giving his services in exchange for board and lodging. But he soon became an able draughtsman with a particular aptitude for making attractive perspective drawings for clients who were not quite sure what they wanted."[26] An invaluable person for an architect to have in his office. "The association between Pugin and Nash lasted for many years, long after Pugin had an office of his own and a reputation as one of the best water-colourists of the day."[27] Nash suggested to Pugin that he should study authentic Gothic buildings and publish an illustrated work that would be of great service to the architectural profession. He was unable to carry out this task single handed. Benjamin Ferrey records that "He therefore sought pupils and readily obtained them, Mr. Nash and other architects being glad to recommend his office as the best school for obtaining a knowledge of Gothic architecture and other elementary branches of art."[28] In 1821 he published his first volume of *Specimens of Gothic Architecture* which he dedicated to Nash as the private architect of the King. To this E. J. Willson contributed the literary part. A second volume followed, "and the work met with a most extensive sale, fully justifying the hopes of its promoters."[29] After this success, "and really animated with a love for mediaeval art, Pugin, to whom the magnificent buildings of Normandy were familiar, determined to illustrate some of the French structures with the precision shown in the works he had just published."[30] He did so, in partnership with John Britton (1771–1857), and in 1831 he published his *Examples of Gothic Architecture*.

His son was brought up in this atmosphere of reverence and affection for Gothic architecture, and inherited his father's talent for drawing. Ferrey, who

The tower of St. Michael, Huyton, Lancashire: an example of the native Gothic tradition of building persisting far into the seventeenth century. The upper part of the tower, with its eight stone pinnacles, was built in 1664. Over a hundred years earlier, in 1555, the church was in a ruinous condition, and repairs were carried out in the sixteenth and seventeenth centuries; but no attempt was made to introduce classical features. (See page 19.) *Drawn by David Owen.*

was an articled pupil in the elder Pugin's office, observes that "he rendered little assistance to his father in the prosecution of his architectural works, as the labour of drawing out the details of building in a strictly geometrical manner from given measurements little suited his active habits or mental energy."[31] Ferrey was two years older than young Pugin; he became his friend and biographer, publishing in 1861 a combined biography of father and son. A much later biography, by Michael Trappes-Lomax, was published in 1933, entitled *Pugin: a Mediaeval Victorian.*[32] They are the fullest and best sources of information about him, but neither succeed in bringing that strange, tortured character to life. Ferrey's *Recollections* is an austere work, a trifle acidulated; Trappes-Lomax's book is warmed by generous admiration and understanding; but still the man escapes. You can recapture the fervour and power of his creative gifts, his towering indignation with the ugliness of the period he lived in, and his immense confidence in the only way it could be put right, from his writings and those brilliant illustrations, which show, far better than words could ever describe, the losses England had incurred through industrialism, the alleged glories of the mediaeval past, and his bright hopes for the future, to be attained by means of a revival of the old crafts and a restoration of the Christian approach to life and art, which would appease the spiritual hunger of mankind. Of course, the logical end of Pugin's belief in the excellence of mediaeval art and life was to embrace the faith that had originally inspired that art and life, and in the mid 1830's he was received into the Roman Church. By this conscientious logic he diminished his powers as a propagandist for the Gothic revival: as a papist he was suspect; the fiery protestor against ugliness was discounted because he was not a Protestant; but nobody, not the most bigoted Anglican, could deny the sincerity of his work, or be oblivious to the passion that inspired his writings.

His energy and activity were immense: he was a superb draughtsman, and produced drawings and sketches of Gothic details, churches, and splendid compositions at great speed, all lit by a sensitive understanding of the spirit of mediaeval art. They were not copies: they were the work of a mind that understood and rejoiced in the methods and ideas and lived in the faith of the mediaeval masons and carvers and builders. He also published satires, as graphically biting as Hogarth's a century before or Osbert Lancaster's a century later. His book of *Contrasts* has been mentioned in Chapter I, and the character of that attack on contemporary life, architecture and industrialism has lost none of its strength today. The illustrations reproduced on pages 23 and 28 prove that. We have, perhaps, a greater sensitivity than our great-grandfathers about the preservation of old buildings and things of beauty, but we possess far more competent and comprehensive facilities for destruction: we have the bulldozer, and, because they are sentient, those even more destructive agents, the speculative builder and the intellectual planner.

Pugin attacked the squalid muddle of early nineteenth-century towns, and the first plate of his *Contrasts*[33] showed a town of 1840 compared with an idealised reconstruction of it in 1440. In the former the greed, inurbanity and bitter ugliness of the early industrial age have replaced the spaciousness and beauty of the mediaeval city. The beauty of the mediaeval city with its soaring spires was undeniable; its spaciousness was a myth, for it was usually the close prisoner of its encircling walls, congested, insanitary, and immeasurably inferior to the great cities of the ancient Graeco-Roman world. Trappes-Lomax admits that Pugin "was not entirely fair in his satire." Adding that "It is hard for a man to be quite fair when he is wholly in earnest."[34] And Pugin was fiercely in earnest; intent, fanatical, humourless. In another book the present writer has observed that those contrasting views were inspired less by a desire for objective criticism than by a passionate sense of loss—loss of beauty and serenity and spiritual significance. To restore such properties to life should be the mission of the Gothic revival—which was only part of the greater mission of reuniting Christendom. In his drawing of an industrialised town of 1840, the buildings reflected the inhumanity of an age that created, and found good, such harsh fantastic chaos. In many parts of modern industrial England, "mediaeval church towers and spires stand in mute reproof of our unlovely materialism, emphasising the comparison between an age of faith and an age of greed, which Pugin found intolerable—the more so because many of his contemporaries were incapable of appreciating what was missing from life."[35] The book of *Contrasts* was a spirited attack not only on the town itself, but upon the component parts, the social institutions that employed architecture, and the classic idiom that was accepted as the respectable and safe solution for secular and sacred buildings. The plates on contrasted crosses attacked the new forces that were beginning to affect everyday life. (See pages 24 and 25.) The illustration of Chichester Cross shows his great ability as a draughtsman, for he could draw Gothic buildings with insight and

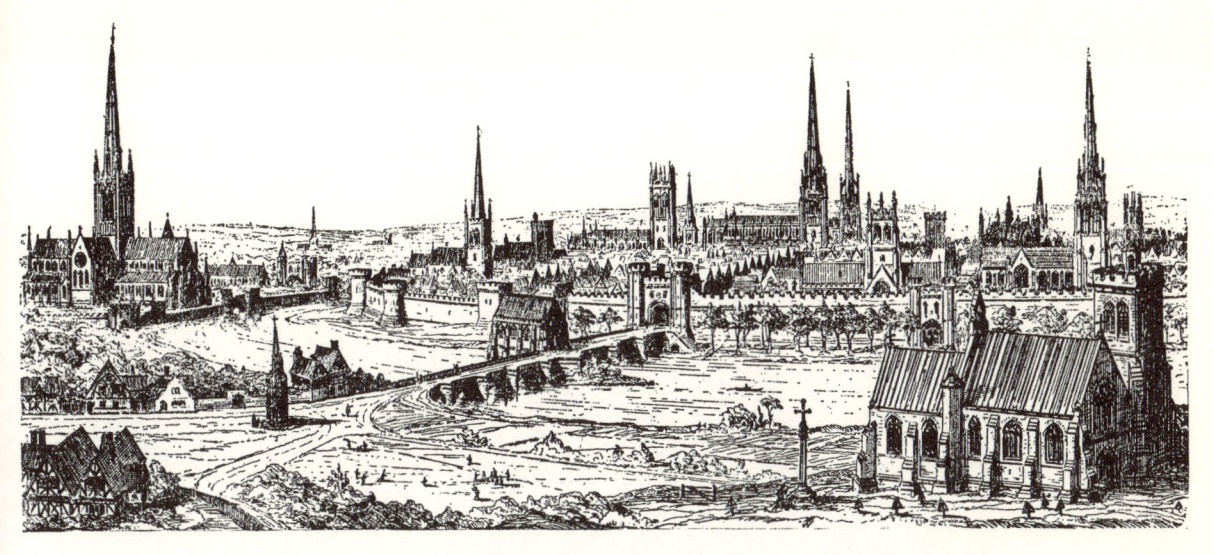

Above: A Catholic town in 1440. *Below:* The same town in 1840. From Pugin's *Contrasts*, second edition, 1841.

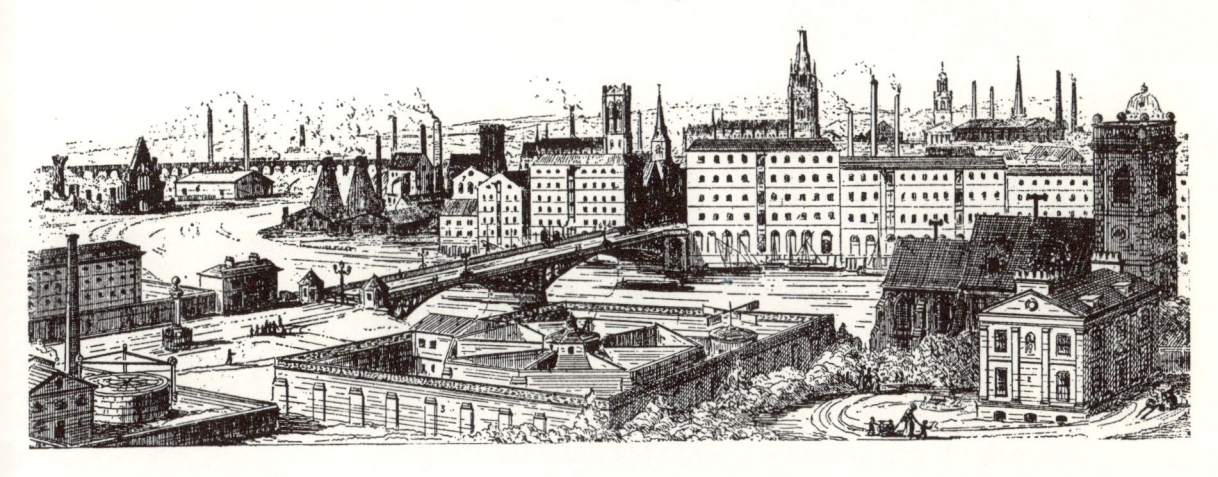

sympathy. As a contrast, he selected King's Cross, Battlebridge, a preposterous monument to George IV, with a police station in the base.

The book of *Contrasts* was first published by the author (at a heavy loss) in 1836, and the year before borough constabulary forces had been established by the Municipal Corporation Act (1835), and Sir Robert Peel's metropolitan police—whose members were known at first as "peelers"—was already in existence. The new force was disliked and suspected by many people. To free Englishmen policemen and municipal officers were visible symbols of a new bureaucratic tyranny. Dickens always mocked them, and gave that

Contrasted Crosses. Chichester Cross, from Pugin's *Contrasts*. Like the views of the two towns on page 23, this drawing illustrates Pugin's ability as a draughtsman, and his sympathetic understanding of Gothic details. (See opposite page.)

dignified embodiment of parochial power, the beadle, a label that made it difficult ever to take beadles seriously again, for who could respect a "Mr. Bumble"? Pugin put both police and municipal officers in the pillory in the plates which showed conduits, and residences for the poor.(36)

In Chapter II of *Contrasts*, Pugin mounted his attack on what he stigmatised as the "revived pagan style." He said it was "time to break the chains of

CHRISTIAN GOTHIC 25

King's Cross, Battle-bridge: a preposterous monument to George IV. It was selected by Pugin as a contrast with the Gothic splendour of Chichester Cross. (See opposite.) This structure, demolished in 1845, was 60 feet high, the statue 11 feet, and the base was used first as a police station, then as a public house with a camera-obscura in the upper storey. The view below, taken during demolition, is from *Old and New London*, Volume II, edited by Walter Thornbury. Chapter XXXIV, page 277. (London: Cassell, Petter & Galpin, 1872–78.)

Paganism which have enslaved the Christians of the last three centuries, and diverted the noblest powers of their minds, from the pursuit of truth to the reproduction of error. Almost all the researches of modern antiquaries, schools of painting, national museums and collections, have only tended to corrupt taste and poison the intellect, by setting forth classic art as the summit of excellence, and substituting mere natural and sensual productions in the place

Contrasted public conduits. The West Cheap Conduit, 1479: opposite, St. Anne's, Soho. From Pugin's *Contrasts*.

of mystical and divine."(37) This was part of his attack on classical architecture and all that it implied in order and lucidity and graciousness. There was no need, he said, for "visiting the distant shores of Greece and Egypt to make discoveries in art. England alone abounds in hidden and unknown antiquities of surpassing interest. What madness, then, while neglecting our own religious and national types of architecture and art, to worship at the revived shrines of ancient corruption and profane the temple of a crucified Redeemer by

Contrasted public conduits. St. Anne's, Soho. From Pugin's *Contrasts*. The chained pump and the stern policeman have replaced the gushing fountain shown opposite. Within twenty years of the publication of *Contrasts* the first public drinking fountain was erected in London.

the architecture and emblems of heathen gods. The Pagan monster, which has ruled so long, and with such powerful sway over the intellects of mankind, is now tottering to its fall; and although its growth is too strong, and its hold too powerful to be readily overthrown, still its hideous form has been unmasked, and the strength of its assailants daily increases."(38)

This championship of the Gothic revival, with its religious sanctions, represented the fanatical minority: larger, and far more influential, because it was

Contrasted residences for the poor. *Left:* An ancient poor house.

Below: A modern poor house. From Pugin's *Contrasts*, second edition, 1841.

less obviously enthusiastic and far more respectable, was the majority of supporters of the Gothic revival, composed of English puritans, who as Evangelicals or Nonconformists, had unostentatiously reassumed the powers they had lost at the Restoration, and were prepared to see that their own families and the people of England were given, as Oliver Cromwell had put it, "not what they want but what is good for them." This emotional fire, stoked by mutually intolerant religious sects, had its temperature increased by the legend of an older and better England, the "Merrie England" legend, fathered by Cobbett, exaggerated by Washington Irving, gravely endorsed by Pugin and Ruskin, embroidered by William Morris, and in our own century produced as a splendid pageant in prose and verse by Hilaire Belloc and Gilbert Keith Chesterton.

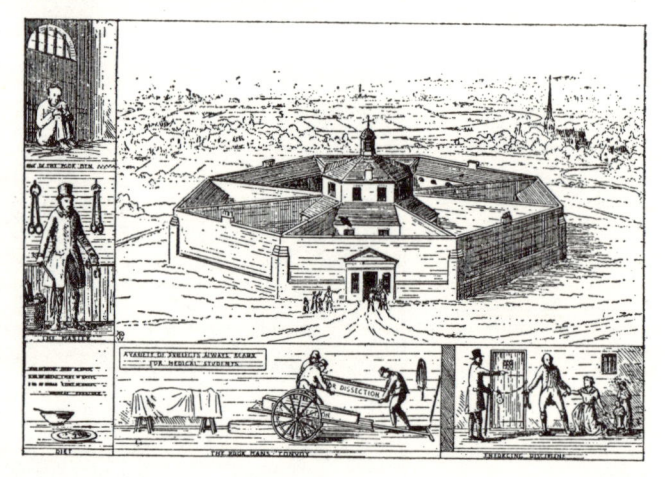

"Love of country," wrote Cobbett, "that variety of feelings which, all together, constitute what we properly call *patriotism*, consist in part of the admiration of, and veneration for, ancient and magnificent proofs of skill and opulence."(39) His theme in *A History of the Protestant Reformation in England and Ireland* was "the good old times," the free, lovely, hospitable England that was destroyed in the middle years of the sixteenth century, reinforced by his defence of pre-Reformation social and monastic institutions. The sincerity of his book is emphasised by the last paragraph where he states: "Born and bred a Protestant of the Church of England, having a wife and numerous family professing the same faith, having the remains of dearly beloved parents lying in a Protestant churchyard, and trusting to conjugal or filial piety to place mine by their side, I have, in this undertaking had no motive, I can have had no motive, but a sincere and disinterested love of truth and justice."[40]

Like Pugin, Cobbett hated injustice, whether it occurred in the past or disfigured the present. He stigmatised the Reformation as "a devastation of England, which was at the time when this event took place, the happiest country, perhaps, that the world had ever seen...."[41] After the pillage of the monasteries and the redistribution of their estates, "The noble buildings, raised in the view of lasting for countless ages; the beautiful gardens; these ornaments of the country must not be suffered to stand, for they continually reminded the people of the rapacity and cruelty of their tyrant and his fellow-plunderers and partakers in the plunder.... In many cases, those who got the estates were bound to destroy the buildings, or to knock them partly down, so that people should, at once, be deprived of all hope of seeing a revival of what they had lost, and in order to give them encouragement to take leases under the *new owners*. The whole country was, thus, disfigured; it had the appearance of a land recently invaded by the most brutal barbarians; and this appearance, if we look well into it, it has even to this day."[42]

The well-ordered Georgian scene; the spacious towns; the great country seats with their parks and groves and gardens; the century and a half of skilful planting, which followed the publication of John Evelyn's *Sylva* in 1664, his famous and best-selling *Discourse of Forest Trees and the Propagation of Timber*; the far-reaching improvements in agriculture and the incentives of long leases to good farming which led up to and followed the work and example of Thomas William Coke, Earl of Leicester (1754–1842), better known as "Coke of Norfolk": all these gains were as nothing to Cobbett, who discoursed on ruins with the eloquence of a Sir Uvedale Price or a Thomas Warton, though without their affection for romantic, picturesque effects. He was concerned only with the economic consequences of the loss of Old England, a disaster which began three centuries before his lament for it was published. "Go into any county and survey," he said, "even at this day, the ruins of its, perhaps, twenty Abbeys and Priories; and, then, ask yourself, 'what have we *in exchange for these*'? Go to the site of some once-opulent Convent. Look at the cloister, now become, in the hands of a rack-renter, the receptacle for dung, fodder and faggot-wood: see the hall, where for ages, the widow, the orphan, the aged and the stranger, found a table ready spread; see a bit of its walls now helping to make a cattle-shed, the rest having been hauled away to build a *workhouse*: recognise, in the side of a barn, a part of the once-magnificent

Chapel: and, if, chained to the spot by your melancholy musings, you be admonished of the approach of night by the voice of the screech-owl, issuing from those arches, which once, at the same hour, resounded with the vespers of the monk, and which have, for seven hundred years, been assailed by storms and tempests in vain; if thus admonished of the necessity of seeking food, shelter, and a bed lift your eyes and look at the white-washed and dry-rotten shell on the hill, called the 'gentleman's house'; and, apprized of the 'board-wages' and the spring-guns, suddenly turn your head; jog away from the scene of devastation; with 'old English Hospitality' in your mind, reach the nearest inn, and there, in room half-warmed and half-lighted, and with reception precisely proportioned to the presumed length of your purse, sit down and listen to an account of the hypocritical pretences, the base motives, the tyrannical and bloody means, under which, from which, and by which, that devastation was effected, and that hospitality banished for ever from the land."[43]

He was particularly incensed by the destruction of monastic establishments in Surrey, the county of his birth, and was "filled with indignation against the ruffian devastators," as formerly the county was "from one end of it to the other, ornamented and benefited by the establishments which grew out of the Catholic Church."[44] After listing them he said: "To these belonged *cells* and *chapels* at a distance from the convents themselves: so that it would have been a work of some difficulty for a man so to place himself, even in this poor, heathy county, at six miles distance from a place where the door of hospitality was always open to the poor, to the aged, the orphan, the widow, and the stranger. Can any man *now* place himself, in that whole county, within any number of miles of any such door? No; nor in any other county. All is wholly changed, and all is changed for the worse. There is now no *hospitality* in England. Words have changed their meaning. We now give entertainment to those who entertain us in return. We entertain people because we *like them personally*; and, very seldom, because they stand in need of entertainment. An *hospital*, in those days, meant a place of free entertainment; and not a place merely for the lame, the sick and the blind; and the very sound of the words, 'Old English Hospitality,' ought to raise a blush on every Protestant cheek. But, besides this hospitality exercised invariably in the monasteries, the weight of their *example* was great with all the opulent classes of the community; and thus, to be generous and kind was the character of the nation at large: a niggardly, a base, a money-loving disposition could not be in fashion, when those institutions to which all men looked with reverence, set an example which condemned such a disposition."[45]

Cobbett died in 1835, the year before Pugin's book of *Contrasts* was published, a work that might almost have been planned as a sequel to *A History of the Protestant Reformation*. Although Pugin intended that it should show "the disastrous effect of the Protestant or destructive principle, on Catholic art

CHRISTIAN GOTHIC 31

St. Marie's Grange, the house Pugin built for himself near Salisbury. His biographer, Benjamin Ferrey, said that "there was nothing very inviting in the exterior design, and a great absence of modern comfort in the interior arrangement. The building tended rather to show the eccentricity of its owner than his superior skill in design. . . ." (From Ferrey's *Recollections*, Chapter VI, pages 72–73.)

and architecture in England,"[46] which it did with a wealth of technical and historical detail in the text and plates, it is doubtful whether a forthright, John Bullish character like Cobbett would have appreciated the dialectical subtlety of the Gothic and Catholic revivalist. Cobbett was a blunt Englishman, handicapped by the "suspicion, which never leaves the ill-educated even when they are brilliantly intelligent, that the man of higher culture is making a fool of them," a defect which caused him to blurt out to Talleyrand, who had "complimented him upon his wit and learning" and politely enquired whether he had been at Oxford or Cambridge, that he "was no trout, and consequently not to be caught by tickling."[47] Duff Cooper, describing that conversation between the great French statesman and the self-schooled, self-made politician and writer who began life as a farmer's boy, observed that Cobbett was incapable of believing that Talleyrand had visited him merely because he wanted to meet a remarkable man.[48]

Cobbett, an unconscious propagandist for the Gothic revival and the much later handicraft revival, fought a rearguard action for the rural England of beef and beer and home handicrafts; not the "Merrie England" of his pre-Reformation dreams; but pre-industrial England, that still existed in his day before the Puritans again rose to power and impoverished the people, proscribed their pleasures, and injured their health in factories and slums. Cobbett denounced all those preachers made in the likeness of Stiggins, whether they were ignorant tricksters or austere Doctors of Divinity. "The doctrines, which fanaticism preaches," he said, "and which teach men to be *content* with *poverty*, have a very pernicious tendency, and are calculated to favour tyrants by giving them passive slaves. To live well, to enjoy all things that make life pleasant, is the right of every man who constantly uses his strength judiciously and lawfully. It is to blaspheme God to suppose, that he created men to be miserable, to hunger, thirst, and perish with cold, in the midst of that abundance which is the fruit of their own labour. Instead, therefore, of applauding '*happy* poverty,' which applause is so much the fashion of the present day, I despise the man that is *poor* and *contented*; for, such content is certain proof of a base disposition, a disposition which is the enemy of all industry, all exertion, all love of independence."[49] He would have despised those acquiescent proletarians, classified by Dr. Thomas Arnold as the "good poor."[50] Cobbett found nothing good in poverty, which, he said "never finds a place among the *blessings* promised by God."[51]

Arnold denounced the moral irresponsibility of industrialism. "A man sets up a factory," he said, "and wants hands. I beseech you to observe the very expressions that are used, for they are all significant. What he wants of his fellow-creatures is the loan of his hands—of their heads and hearts he thinks nothing. These hands are attached to certain mouths and bodies which must be fed and lodged; but this must be done as cheaply as possible. . . . But further, these hands are attached to reasonable minds and to immortal souls. The mouths and bodies must be provided for, however miserably, because without them the hands cannot work; but the minds and souls go utterly unregarded. Is this other than a national crime?"[52] He was attacking the moral neglect of the industrialists for their workpeople, but apparently accepted the cheap and shoddy feeding and housing of factory operatives, believing perhaps that there was an affirmative answer to Blake's lines:

"And was Jerusalem builded here
Among these dark Satanic mills?"

Pugin's town of 1840, with its ruined and mutilated churches, its brutal ugliness, its industrial buildings, and the various edifices that accommodated what one of Marryat's characters called "free trade in religion,"[53] was the architectural result of *laissez-faire*, the Manchester School individualism that was to minister so soothingly to Victorian comfort. Pugin was as intolerant of the society which produced such aesthetic barbarities as he was of the social consequences, and his drawing of contrasted residences for the poor (page 28) might have been used as illustrations for Cobbett's description of monastic hospitality. It was inconceivable, to his mind, that any form of architecture, other than Gothic, could be acceptable to a Christian society; he had no illusions about the acquisitive, respectable society surrounding his own bright island of inspired reaction. His isolation was protected and sustained by his own blazing faith, and he was convinced not only of the iniquity of paganism in architecture, but of its superlative silliness. His case against the use of the classic orders he condensed into this sentence: "Christian art," he said, "was the natural result of the progress of Catholic feeling and devotion; and its decay was consequent on that of the faith itself; and all revived classic buildings, whether erected in Catholic or Protestant countries, are evidences of a lamentable departure from true Catholic principles and feelings. . . ."[54]

His book on *The True Principles of Pointed or Christian Architecture*, issued in

Christchurch, Herne Bay, an unpretentious Gothic structure, completed in 1841. It was the sort of design that fitted in admirably with the classic façades of the terraces and squares that were built in the early days of the seaside resort. Pugin wrote in 1841: "Let every man build to God according to his means, but not practise showy deceptions: better is it to do a little substantially and consistently with truth, than to produce a great but fictitious effect." (*The True Principles of Pointed or Christian Architecture*, page 45.) Although Pugin was attacking the sort of falsity and pretentiousness he illustrated in a later part of his book, which is shown below (reproduced from page 57), the design of Christchurch, Herne Bay, was too closely related to eighteenth-century fashions to please an ardent missionary of the Gothic Revival. Pugin and Ruskin had even less use for "gentlemen's Gothic" than they had for the classic orders of architecture. (See pages 9 and 16.)

1841, set forth two basic principles for design which were: "1st, there should be no features about a building which are not necessary for convenience, construction, or propriety; 2nd, that all ornament should consist of enrichment of the essential construction of a building."[55] Two years later, Pugin published *An Apology for the Revival of Christian Architecture*, with a few illustrations in the bitter spirit of his *Contrasts* and a striking frontispiece in which twenty-five of his designs were assembled, like some celestial city—a vision of towers, spires and steep roofs with urgently ascending lines. How different in spirit and execution from Cockerell's famous drawing of Wren's principal buildings in a single group, exhibited at the Royal Academy in 1838. Side by side those drawings epitomise the Ages of Faith and Reason. (See frontispiece.)

Pugin hoped that the Age of Faith could be restored. "The age in which we live," he wrote, "is a most eventful period for English art. We are just emerging from a state which may be termed the dark ages of architecture. After a gradual decay of four centuries, the style—for style there was—became so execrably bad, that the cup of degradation was filled to the brim; and as taste had fallen to its lowest depth, a favourable reaction commenced. The breaking up of this wretched state of things has naturally produced a complete convulsion in the whole system of arts, and a Babel of confusion has succeeded to the one bad idea that generally prevailed.

"Private judgment runs riot; every architect has a theory of his own, a beau ideal he has himself created; a disguise with which to invest the building he erects. This is generally the result of his latest travels. One breathes nothing but the Alhambra—another the Parthenon—a third is full of lotus cups and pyramids from the banks of the Nile—a fourth, from Rome, is all dome and basilica; whilst another works Stuart and Revett on a modified plan, and builds lodges, centenary chapels, reading-rooms, and fish-markets, with small Doric work and white brick facings. Styles are now *adopted* instead of *generated*, and ornament and design *adapted to*, instead of *originated by*, the edifices themselves.

"This may, indeed, be appropriately termed the *carnival* of architecture; its professors appear tricked out in the guises of all centuries and all nations; the Turk and the Christian, the Egyptian and the Greek, the Swiss and the Hindoo, march side by side, and mingle together; and some of these gentlemen, not satisfied with perpetrating one character, appear in two or three costumes in the same evening! Amid this motley group (oh! miserable degradation!) the venerable form and sacred detail of our national and Catholic architecture may be discerned; but *how* adopted? Not on consistent principle, not on authority, not as the expression of our faith, our government, or country, but as one of the disguises of the day, to be put on and off at pleasure, and used occasionally as circumstances or private caprice may suggest."[56]

Pugin saw arising about him the Gothic of the copybooks, the forms and ornamental details taken from Loudon's *Encyclopaedia* and other sources, reliable and otherwise. And being an architect, not merely a writer or lecturer on architecture, or an *architecturalist*—a Victorian word coined to describe a professed student or connoisseur of architecture—he was disgusted with all this shallow imitative stuff whether it pretended to be Gothic or classic. He returned to the basic principles of architectural design. "To advocate Christian architecture merely on the score of its beauty," he said, "can never prevail with those who profess to think that all art and majesty is concentrated in a Grecian temple. We must turn to the principles from which all styles have originated. The history of architecture is the history of the world; as we inspect the edifices of antiquity, its nations, its dynasties, its religions, are all brought before us. The belief and manners of all people are embodied in the edifices they raised; it was impossible for any of them to have built consistently otherwise than they did: each was the inventor and perfecter of their peculiar style; each style was the type of their Religion, customs, and climate."[57]

He wondered whether the architecture of his time, "even supposing it solid enough to last," would reveal to posterity "any certain clue or guide to the system under which it was erected." He thought not, because it failed to express "existing opinions and circumstances," disclosing instead, "a confused jumble of styles and symbols borrowed from all nations and periods. Are not the adapters of pagan architecture violating every principle, that regulated the men whose works they profess to imitate?" he asked. "These uncompromising advocates of classic styles would be utterly repudiated by the humblest architect of pagan antiquity, were he now to return to earth. Vitruvius would spew if he beheld the works of those who glory in calling him master." He thought that "The restorers of Christian architecture are more consistent followers of classic *principles* than all these boasted Greeks; they understand antiquity, and apply the ancient consistent rules to the new dispensation. The moderns, in their pretended imitation of the classic system, are constantly producing the greatest anomalies; and we are called upon to admire their thrice-cooked hashes of pagan fragments (in which the ingredients are amalgamated in utter confusion) as fine national monuments of the present age."[58]

Every achievement of the Renaissance was swept aside, for, like Ruskin, he felt that the great rebirth of classical learning and architecture was a spiritual misdemeanour; a moral aberration, disastrous alike to Europe and England. "The change which took place in the sixteenth century," he believed, "was not a matter of mere taste, but a change of soul; it was a great contention between Christian and pagan ideas, in which the latter triumphed, and for the first time *inconsistency* in architectural design was developed." He described some of the inconsistencies exhibited by Renaissance churches. As for contemporary public buildings, there was not, he asserted, "one edifice of the whole number that is not painful to contemplate as a monument of national art."[59] He excepted the New Houses of Parliament, on which he had collaborated with Sir Charles Barry (1795–1860).

Barry had won the first premium in the competition for the new building in 1836; there had been ninety-seven competitors; and the required style was "Gothic or Elizabethan." Externally the building was the antithesis of Christian architecture, but gained its rich, impressive character from the cross-fertilisation of two cultures, classic and Gothic, and the result was as unmistakably English in feeling as the pre-Renaissance architecture of the early Tudor period. When it was in course of erection, before the towers were added, Pugin had observed to a friend: "All Grecian, Sir; Tudor details on a classic body."[60] Although the design was classic in inspiration, Pugin refrained from calling it pagan; possibly because it was not a place of worship, perhaps because he thought the purity of the mediaeval ornament redressed the classical heresy of form.

Originally, Barry had hired Pugin as a "ghost," but soon found himself battling with an impulsive and industrious genius whose abilities transcended those of a mere anonymous assistant: the "ghost" materialised and became an acknowledged collaborator.[61] Despite disputes and disagreements, and an interval of seven years when Pugin abandoned the collaboration, and had to be coaxed back, Barry generously acknowledged his debt to the inspired help he received,[62] and Pugin was eventually "appointed to aid in the great national undertaking. The designing of the internal fittings, furniture, decoration, encaustic floors, &c., were officially confided to him, and to his unremitting energy and attention in the formation and selection of carvers, glass-stainers, metal-workers, &c., &c., may be attributed the great excellence and beauty here attained, as well as the masterly skill shown by him in their conception."[63] (See plate 23.)

During his lifetime Pugin communicated his passion for Christian Gothic to many discerning patrons; his opportunities to build increased and multiplied, and he erected over sixty-five churches in the United Kingdom and many overseas in the Colonies. He built convents, monasteries, schools and large houses, and the demonic activity of his short life, particularly during the last years, ended in madness. The impact of his work and writings affected both the architectural profession and the educated public, and he was praised, admired, and savagely criticised, but never ignored. Ruskin, with the irascible arrogance for which he was infamous, and obviously regarding himself as the Protestant champion of Christian Gothic, said that Pugin was not a great architect, "but one of the smallest possible or conceivable architects" and concluded an intemperate attack on his work with these words:

"I am sorry to have to speak thus of any living architect; and there is much in this man, if he were rightly estimated, which we might both regard and profit by. He has a most sincere love for his profession, a hearty honest enthusiasm for pixes and piscinas; and though he will never design a pix or a piscina thoroughly well, yet better than most of the experimental architects of the day. Employ him by all means, but on small work. Expect no cathedrals of him; but no one, at present, can design a better finial. That is an exceedingly

The Victoria Tower, completed in 1860. The Houses of Parliament were designed by Sir Charles Barry (1795–1860) and built between 1840 and 1868, the work being finished, after Barry's death, by his son, E. M. Barry. A. W. N. Pugin was an active and influential collaborator. (See pages 35 and 36 also plate 23.) *Drawn by A. S. Cook.*

beautiful one over the west door of St. George's; and there is some spirited impishness and switching of tails in the supporting figures at the imposts. Only do not allow his good designing of finials to be employed as an evidence in matters of divinity, nor thence deduce the incompatibility of Protestantism and art."

Ferrey, after quoting this attack, said: "The withering sarcasm of these remarks can scarcely be said to be warranted under any circumstances. It so far exceeds the bounds of fairness, that thoughtful people feel shocked at finding a man of Ruskin's ability descending to such gross personalities, in order to embody in them the expression of his bitter aversion to Romanism."[64]

Ruskin frequently descended to gross personalities, until the bubble of his pontifical reputation as a critic of painting was pricked by Whistler in 1878. But as a master of ornate prose he roused and sustained popular enthusiasm for the Gothic Revival, and was as sincerely distressed as Pugin to see how successfully commercial Gothic competed with Christian Gothic, and how many architects built up huge practices by exploiting the emotional credulity of their patrons, who accepted as pure mediaeval spirit some very doubtful concoctions. John T. Emmett, one of the few discerning Victorian critics of architecture, writing in 1875, described the degradation of Christian Gothic. "The churches that have been 'religiously' designed by the 'Profession' during the last thirty years," he said, "are ghastly imitations, true perhaps in style and in material, but in art a stultifying manufacture, made especially to please; and then professionally palmed upon the clergy, and received as elevating and 'religious' truth."[65]

Meanwhile hundreds of Gothic churches and secular buildings had been built all over Britain. The Gothic Revival coincided with a series of great architectural competitions; for the Houses of Parliament in 1835, the Government Offices in Whitehall in 1856, and the Law Courts in 1866. Municipal authorities were erecting town halls and offices; wealthy manufacturers were building castles and Elizabethan and Jacobean mansions; Gothic had also to compete with a revived Byzantine style, and with all the Italianate fancies that occurred to architects who favoured the classic side in the Battle of the Styles. Architecture had become, as Pugin had said, "a confused jumble of styles and symbols borrowed from all nations and periods." The Age of Faith had not been restored: the plutocracy and the middle classes, who called the tune, were far too comfortable to be Christians, and as usual architecture reflected their character as patrons, their ebullient prosperity, their artistic bankruptcy, and abounding self-satisfaction. What began as a Holy War ended, like many another missionary enterprise, in commercial exploitation. First, the pure milk of the Word—then trade gin.

CHAPTER IV

LOUDON AND DOWNING

COMMERCIAL Gothic had its priests and prophets; not only architects who took themselves and their work with great seriousness, but industrious compilers of copy books, whose influence spread throughout the United Kingdom and the Colonies, and inspired imitators in the United States. John Claudius Loudon (1783–1843) in Britain, and Andrew Jackson Downing (1815–52) in America, were the most prolific of these compilers: their careers were in many ways comparable, and as landscape gardeners, horticulturalists and—to a lesser extent—practising architects, they exerted, through their published works, considerable influence on the buildings of both countries, particularly in rural areas. Both were concerned with the broadest interpretation of the architect's responsibility, and in their books they covered the laying-out of grounds, the planning and building of mansions and cottages, and their interior decoration and furnishing. Downing owed much to Loudon's books, and generously acknowledged the debt, for Loudon's best-selling *Encyclopaedia of Cottage, Farm, and Villa Architecture and Furniture*, first issued in 1833, was well known in the United States. Before its publication, Loudon had been in correspondence with American publishers about the distribution of prospectuses, and had 5,000 printed for insertion in magazines.[66] Downing edited the first American edition of Mrs. Loudon's *Gardening for Ladies*.

Loudon was the son of a Scottish farmer, of Kerse Hall, Gogar, near Edinburgh. Like many other Scots he went to England as a young man to seek his fortune, and actually made one, which he lost, and a reputation, which he retained. It was a curiously diverse reputation, for his energy and versatility were about equally matched. This variously accomplished man, who was almost a genius, probably missed greatness by attempting to do too much too quickly. He was dedicated to work, and despite crippling physical disabilities, was immensely industrious: he was also arrogant, humourless, morally confident in the rectitude of his opinions and tastes, insatiably curious and interested in everything, and died at the age of sixty from overwork and worry. The material he collected and edited provides an illuminating record of the transitional period in architecture and design between late Georgian and early Victorian. He lived a full life, and published many works, now almost forgotten, save the *Encyclopaedia of Cottage, Farm, and Villa Architecture and Furniture*,

Double detached suburban villa, in Porchester Terrace, Bayswater, front elevation. In the right-hand house, Loudon lived and had his office. Side elevation below.

From Loudon's *The Suburban Gardener and Villa Companion* (1838), pages 325–29. See plate 6 for present-day view of the house, also plate 18.

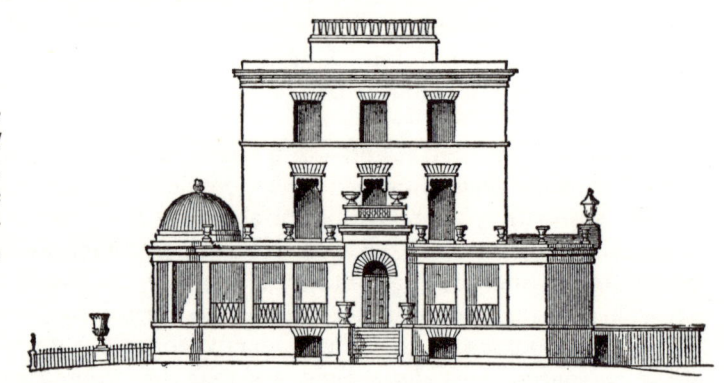

which gave a pre-view of Victorian taste, and the *Arboretum Britannicum*, which ruined him financially. He could be described as an habitual encyclopaedist; for in addition to his best known and most profitable work, already mentioned, he produced in 1822 an *Encyclopaedia of Gardening*, in two volumes, followed in 1825 by an *Encyclopaedia of Agriculture*, also in two volumes, an *Encyclopaedia of Plants* in 1829, and an *Encyclopaedia of Trees and Shrubs* in 1842. He was primarily interested in gardening, particularly landscape gardening, and in the first decade of the nineteenth century had established certainly one of the earliest, if not the first, agricultural college in England, at Tew Park, Oxfordshire. These activities aroused a corresponding interest in architecture, and one of his earliest known works was the remodelling of Wood Hall Farm, Pinner, in Middlesex, described and illustrated in a book, published in 1812, that he dedicated to the Prince Regent.[67] Loudon's father took on the lease of Wood Hall Farm in 1807, and his son transformed the rather rambling farmhouse of a type common enough in the sixteenth and seventeenth centuries, so it became a bright, pleasant, whitewashed house which exhibited some Georgian characteristics, and was typical of many small country houses and detached suburban villas built in the first half of the nineteenth century, and later. (See plate 6.) His most interesting domestic building was a semi-detached suburban villa in Porchester Terrace, Bayswater, which was then almost a rural area north of the Oxford Road. This became his residence and office, where he spent the last years of his life. The house, No. 3, still stands, and faithfully follows the drawings and specifications Loudon gave in great detail in *The Suburban Gardener and Villa Companion*, which he published in 1838. Following the classical tradition, it was the prototype of innumerable semi-detached suburban houses. An unusual feature of the design was the domical conservatory that united the two houses on the ground floor and was shared by the inhabitants. The glazed dome illustrates the curvilinear technique of glazing that Loudon had perfected after various experiments. (See opposite page and plate 18.) Potentially an inventive designer, he never fully developed his gifts, though he improved the structure of conservatories and hothouses. He invented a wrought-iron sash-bar or glazing bar which could be bent in any direction without diminishing its strength, and this made the glazed curvilinear roof a practical possibility. His invention of what he called "ridge and furrow" glazing for roof construction was used subsequently by Paxton and Decimus Burton in the great glasshouse at Chatsworth, and later by Paxton for the Crystal Palace. (See plate 18.)

Loudon's interest in the design of hothouses was first roused by a paper read before the Horticultural Society in 1815 by Sir George Mackenzie, "On the Form which the Glass of a Forcing-house ought to have, in order to receive the greatest possible quantity of Rays from the Sun." Certain of Mackenzie's suggestions conflicted with Loudon's own ideas, and caused him to make a series of experiments with different kinds of roofs for hothouses, and in 1817 he wrote and published *Remarks on the Construction of Hothouses*, which he dedicated to Sir Joseph Banks, the veteran President of the Royal Society. This was followed, in 1818, by *A Comparative View of the Common and Curvilinear Modes of Roofing Hothouses*, and a pamphlet, *Sketches of Curvilinear Hothouses, with a Description of the various Purposes in Horticultural and General Architecture, to which a Solid Iron Sash Bar (lately invented) is Applicable*. This work includes many sketches of the experimental hothouses Loudon erected at Bayswater, and some of them forecast the character of the Crystal Palace. (See page 42.) Loudon explained that he was anxious to make English hothouses look beautiful in their own right, instead of being mere lean-to sheds. Paxton was acquainted with Loudon and his wife; and was referred to by Mrs. Loudon in her *Memoir* of her husband's life, as "our kind friend, Mr. Paxton"; and it is at least probable that Loudon discussed his structural experiments for greenhouses with the future designer of the Crystal Palace.[68]

His acquaintance with Paxton began after a visit to Chatsworth, during Paxton's absence, when Loudon published some severe views on the layout and upkeep of the gardens, drawing on his considerable reserve of self-righteousness,

Experimental glass roofs erected by Loudon in 1818 at his house in Bayswater, illustrating the curvilinear principle. They were, he believed, the first roofs of this type attempted in Britain. They were included in his pamphlet, issued in 1818 and entitled: *Sketches of Curvilinear Hothouses, with a Description of the various Purposes in Horticultural and General Architecture, to which a Solid Iron Sash Bar (lately invented) is Applicable.* This diagram foreshadows the form both of the great glasshouse at Chatsworth (begun in 1836), and the Palm House at Kew (begun in 1844), by Decimus Burton and Richard Turner. (See plates 18 and 19.)

which made his critical remarks particularly galling to the man responsible. Paxton replied vigorously, and from this acrimonious exchange something like mutual respect arose, for although Loudon certainly deserved Miss Violet Markham's description of "a horticultural John Knox, who went about 'reproving princes in high places' and telling everybody how very unsatisfactory their gardens were," Paxton was far too great a man to bear malice or to ignore Loudon's real abilities. Miss Markham, in her biography of her grandfather, *Paxton and the Bachelor Duke*, has described the first contact between these two very different characters, and has supplemented it by saying that Loudon's attack on the Chatsworth gardens "was really one of the instances which prove that Paxton was the least quarrelsome of men, because a very warm *rapprochement* took place between them; and after Loudon died it was Paxton who principally concerned himself with raising the pension of Loudon's widow."[69]

Loudon was far in advance of his time. London as a city gained greatly in amenities, following a suggestion he made as early as 1803 in his first article, published in the *Literary Journal*, entitled, "Observations on Laying out the Public Squares of London." He disapproved of the mournful evergreens which then grew in nearly all London squares, and suggested that the plane, sycamore and almond would be less depressingly affected by the smoky atmosphere of the city; by the middle of the nineteenth century his suggestion was widely adopted, and those trees were flourishing in almost every square. In the

Gardener's Magazine, which he first produced in 1826 and remained in circulation until his death, he made various proposals, then considered revolutionary, or at least daringly novel. There should, he said, be a band in Kensington Gardens every week, with seats provided so that people could listen to it in comfort. He suggested building "small stone lodges with fire-places at the principal garden gates, for the comfort of doorkeepers in winter." He also suggested that landed proprietors should provide cottages on their estates for their gardeners and other regular labourers on the land.

In 1829 he printed a paper entitled *Parochial Institutions; or an outline of a plan for a National Education Establishment, suitable to the children of All Ranks, from Infancy to the Age of Puberty*. In this he said (i) that parents should be obliged to send their children to school; (ii) that education should be the same for the children of all social classes; (iii) that costs should be paid for, partly at least, out of local rates and taxes; (iv) that public lectures should be held in the schoolhouse in the evenings, for the benefit of adults; (v) that there should be a garden, and grounds for exercise and recreation, attached to each school building. Loudon was one of the earliest advocates of green zones or belts, which he described as "breathing zones or unoccupied places, half a mile broad, at different intervals around London."

Glass dome, 100 feet in diameter and 60 feet high, erected at Bretton Hall, Yorkshire, in 1827. All the perpendicular supports were of cast-iron, and the sash-bar ribs of the roof of wrought-iron. The upper dome was supported independently by cast-iron pillars. The structure was taken down in 1832. From Loudon's *Encyclopaedia* (1833), Sec. 1961, Fig. 1732, pages 980–81. (See plate 18.)

In Volume III of the *Gardener's Magazine* for 1828 he included under "Hints for Improvements" a long review of a novel published the previous year. Written anonymously and containing some prophetic suggestions, it was entitled *The Mummy! A Tale of the Twenty-Second Century*. Loudon was anxious to meet the author, and in February 1830 he was invited to a party at which the unknown novelist was to be present. He discovered that the author was Miss Jane Webb, aged twenty-three. The following September they were married.

The Mummy! pictured England as Jane Webb imagined it might be four hundred years hence. Her description of various appliances and habits have a strong likeness to many things that are now accepted parts of our environment. For example, she predicted mattresses made of elastic springs; a form of air conditioning, operated by means of tubes "for withdrawing the decomposed air, and admitting fresh," and by ventilators in the ceilings, and ". . . a patent coffee-machine, by which coffee was roasted, ground, made, and poured out with an *ad libitum* of boiling milk and sugar, all in the short space of five minutes. . . ." Mass production of clothes had been perfected, for coats were "woven in machines, where the wool is stripped off the sheep's back at one end, and the coat comes out completely made, in the newest fashion, at the other." The dead were never buried in or near places of worship, but in cemeteries outside the towns.[70]

Loudon referred to many of these customs and inventions when he reviewed the book in the *Gardener's Magazine*. "Communications are held with every part of the world by means of telegraphs. . . . A steam digging machine is mentioned; cooking is effected by a chemical preparation, without the use of fire. . . . Water is turned into ice by mechanical pressure; fog and vapour is turned into snow or rain at pleasure, by withdrawing electricity; all travelling is performed in balloons; the tour of the whole world can be made in six weeks. . . . The country is governed by an absolute queen, who is 'full of wild-goose schemes.' . . ." These included "a plan for making aerial bridges to convey heavy weights from one steeple to another; a machine for stamping shoes and boots at one blow out of a solid piece of leather; a steam-engine for milking cows; and an elastic summer-house, that might be folded up so as to be put into a man's pocket."

Jane Webb had produced two other books before her marriage, *Prose and Verse* in 1824, and *Stories of a Bride* in 1829; but she subsequently became known, and indeed famous, as an authoress of horticultural and botanical works. These she began to write a few years after her marriage. She accompanied Loudon on nearly all his travels at home and in Europe, for both before and after marriage he was a great traveller, and in 1832, when he began the huge task represented by the *Encyclopaedia of Cottage, Farm, and Villa Architecture and Furniture*, she recorded her share in that work. "I was," she wrote, "his sole amanuensis, though he had several draughtsmen. The labour that attended this work was immense; and for several months he and I used to sit up the greater part of every night, never having more than four hours' sleep, and drinking strong coffee to keep ourselves awake." It was diligently illustrated by John Robertson, an architect who had worked as a draughtsman in Loudon's office since 1829.

Throughout the 1830's Loudon's literary activities were unceasing. He seemed to have turned himself into a machine for producing works of reference. He had a flair for picking good contributors to his magazines. In 1838 he was publishing articles on "The Poetry of Architecture," by John Ruskin, then aged nineteen, in *The Architectural Magazine and Journal of Improvement in Architecture, Building and Furnishing and in the various Arts and Trades connected therewith*; an ambitious periodical which Loudon had started four years earlier. He wrote to Ruskin's father, and said, "Your son is the greatest natural genius that ever it has been my fortune to become acquainted with." Ruskin's articles appeared under the pseudonym of Kata Phusin; and Loudon had published in the *Magazine of Natural History* an essay, written when he was fifteen, on the strata of mountains and an enquiry regarding the colour of the Rhine.

Although no word of criticism is to be found in Jane Loudon's memoir of her husband, it is apparent that work during the last twelve years of his life became an obsession; he was prepared to sacrifice anything, and perhaps anybody, in the interests of the tasks that he set for himself. The record of his activities between 1830 and the year of his death supplies the evidence for what amounted to a mania for work. Not all of it was remunerative work; much was disinterested—undertaken and carried through because Loudon felt that some gap in knowledge existed, in the particular fields in which he was a specialist, and therefore that gap had to be filled. He never had a shadow of doubt about his competence to fill in such gaps; so he recorded and indexed, and paraphrased earlier works and earlier findings. His ideas, always racing ahead of his own time, were not the extravagant fancies of a dreamer; they were firmly based upon his own technical knowledge of building and planning; and he

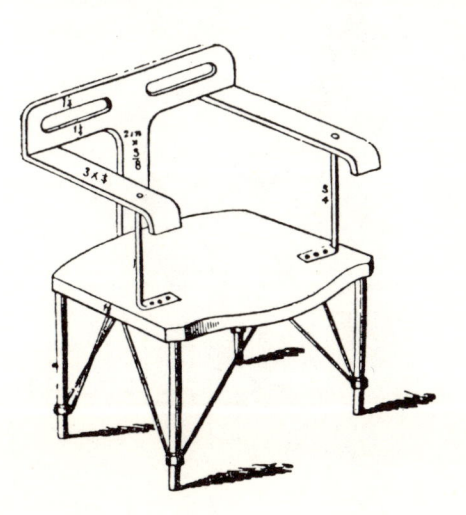

Design for an iron elbow kitchen chair, by Robert Mallet. "The back and elbows are cast in one piece; the supports for the elbows and also the legs are of gas tubing, screwed into a cross frame of iron, which proceeds from the back of the chair under the wooden seat." Loudon's *Encyclopaedia*, Furniture for Cottage Dwellings, page 320.
(See page 47.)

THREE TYPES OF PUBLIC HOUSE

Right: A "Hedge Alehouse" of the smallest size.

Left: A suburban public house in the Old English Style.
Below: A small country inn, with stabling, skittle-ground, tea-garden, and bowling-green. From Loudon's *Encyclopaedia*, pages 680, 687 and 690.

Inside of the counter of the bar room in the "Old English" suburban public house shown on the centre of the opposite page. It illustrates the type of equipment in use, with a "six-motion beer-machine" and a fountain (r) with twelve cocks. From Loudon's *Encyclopaedia*, page 689.

was one of the first technicians in those fields who realised the social implications of architecture, in the broadest sense of the word social. He attracted contributors who were like minded, and to many young men he gave an opportunity of expressing innovating audacities in print. Some of them, like Ruskin, became very great men: others achieved fame as architects or engineers, and of these Robert Mallet was perhaps the best known. He contributed designs and specifications for furniture in cast- and wrought-iron to the *Encyclopaedia of Cottage, Farm, and Villa Architecture and Furniture*, when he was a young man of twenty-three, and suggested using such materials for chairs for cottages and inns, with a courageous independence of prototypes. He was born in Dublin in 1810, the son of John Mallet, a Devonshire man who had settled in Dublin as an iron, brass and copper founder. Robert was trained as an engineer, and built the Fastnet Rock Lighthouse in 1848–49.

The sections on the design and furnishing of inns in the *Encyclopaedia* gave Loudon scope for expressing many ideas that have since been accepted, but were then novel. Unfortunately, the designs he suggested for such places were conceived as imitations of something "old English." The furniture, mainly of cast-iron, reflected the prevailing taste for so-called Gothic ornamentation. Even young Robert Mallet, boldly experimenting with cast-iron and tubular metal for chairs, also supplied suggestions for Gothic table ends and brackets and chairs. Inn furniture of this type is still with us: cast-iron is an enduring material. (See page 152). Many of Loudon's suggestions for inn architecture are with us too, for his *Encyclopaedia* became the principal copy-book for builders all over the country for at least fifty years after it was first published.

Although Loudon was, like so many of his contemporaries, a purveyor of architectural styles, his basic ideas about design and the principles of taste were blameless, though if they were judged only by the illustrations he chose for

GRECIAN AND OLD SCOTS

Left: A small Grecian villa or casino, to be placed on an eminence, commanding extensive prospects in two directions only. From Loudon's *Encyclopaedia*, Design XIII, page 878.

Right: "A villa in the Old Scotch Style, erected in 1831, at Springfield, near Glasgow." Loudon included this example, although he did not altogether approve of it. "Every one who has seen the house of a Scotch laird, erected during the seventeenth century, will allow that this is a very good imitation of the old Scotch manner, which, like the laird himself, was dignified but severe, and forbidding rather than inviting. There is something too commonplace and town-like in the iron rails and the sunk area; and, though porches were unknown to the old Scotch villa, yet the architect would have been perfectly justified in adding one to this Design, provided, in doing so, he adhered to the general style, and manner of building." He observed that "Mr. Cleland may wish his villa to be taken for a real old Scotch house; in which case nothing that is not generally found in such houses should be introduced. This, however, is a low style of art, and is to original composition in Architecture what portrait painting is to historical painting; drawing from an individual instead of from a species. Any builder may copy a style, but it requires an architect to compose in it." He concluded with this revealing opinion: "One reason why churches afford so little pleasure as architectural compositions, in proportion to their great cost, is, that they are, for the most part, facsimiles of one another; or, at any rate, that they are more so than any other class of buildings, public or private, whatsoever." *Encyclopaedia*, Design XIV, pages 879–80.

such works as the *Encyclopaedia of Cottage, Farm, and Villa Architecture and Furniture* and *The Suburban Gardener and Villa Companion*, he might be written off as an obliging and well-stocked shop-keeper, issuing catalogues or, when called upon, ready with the usual patter: "We can show you some very tasty things in Gothic, Sir, or, if you prefer Classical designs, we have those too, and a rich assortment of Italian modes, Swiss also, if you wish for them." In the same book, *The Suburban Gardener*, he could illustrate and describe an array of such lifeless patterns and also set down his own version of Vitruvian principles of design, paraphrasing Wootton's *Elements of Architecture*, by writing: "The Fitness of a Building for the End in View, ought not only to be real, but apparent."

On paper his aesthetic judgment was usually sound and well balanced; and like so many writers during the first half of the nineteenth century, he took an earnest delight in analysing art and taste. He affirmed that there were principles, common to architecture and gardening, which he described as fine arts, and, as he said, "In order to render this subject as plain as possible, it may be advisable to commence by endeavouring to point out what a fine art is."(71) There is a foretaste of Ruskin in Loudon's examinations of the implications of the various terms which he records as synonymous with fine art. Among these, he mentions "elegant art, art of imagination, art of imitation, art of taste, art of design, art of beauty; and each of these terms is applied to architecture, landscape-gardening, painting, sculpture, and music. One quality, common to all the terms, is the word art; and another is understood, viz. that the end of that art is to please."

He then discussed artificiality in appearance, and took over eight hundred words to say what Lethaby condensed into one memorable sentence: "Art is never artifice." But Loudon lacked the gift of creating a memorable phrase: he wrote with industry, with a sense of moral responsibility, and without a gleam of lightheartedness. What he selected for inclusion in his *Encyclopaedia*, and what he said about the things he chose, reveal much about the advanced decay of taste in the early 1830's. For many years after the author's death, the words "let's look it up in Loudon" must have been used constantly in architects' and builders' offices. The effect of a widespread reliance on the *Encyclopaedia* was marked, and all over Britain the drawings that thronged its pages were used as models. Lodges and gate houses, cottages, farm buildings, stables and outhouses, acquired their character from Loudon's pages. He was sometimes critical of what he described and illustrated but nevertheless included it, thus simplifying the task of the speculative builder who wanted something Gothic or Italianate to imitate cheaply. The examples he gave of villas and cottages in what he called the "castellated style" were perfect illustrations of the commercialised Gothic which Pugin attacked in *The True Principles of Pointed or Christian Architecture*. "What can be more absurd than houses built in what is termed the castellated style?" Pugin asked. "Castellated architecture originated in the wants consequent on a certain state of society: of course the

Five-roomed house, in the "Old English style," to be built of stone, in regular courses, or of brick. Loudon's *Encyclopaedia*, Design XXXI, pages 108 and 110.

Five-roomed cottage, with thick walls, "built of rubble-work," and a slate roof. *Encyclopaedia*, Design LXVII, pages 209 and 211.

necessity of great strength, and the means of defence suited to the military tactics of the day, dictated to the builders of ancient castles the most appropriate style for their construction. Viewed as historical monuments, they are of surprising interest, but as models for our imitation they are worse than useless. What absurdities, what anomalies, what utter contradictions do not the builders of modern castles perpetrate!"[72]

Loudon's directions for building "A Villa for a small Family" in this mock-mediaeval manner showed his innocent unconsciousness of their absurdity. "The *situation* for a villa in this style," he wrote, "according to general associations, should be on a bold, commanding rocky prominence, where it might be supposed that, in some former period, a baronial castle for actual defence may have been placed. It is not necessary on that account, however, that it should be accompanied by fortified outworks; but still the terrace-walls, and other ornamental architectural appendages which accompany it, should either be in some degree marked by the lines and finish of fortified walls, or should imitate their ruins. Even, in point of architectural harmony, the crests (tops) of such walls should be more or less embattled, like the parapets of the house. A slight degree of acquaintance with Military Architecture, or with the existing ruins of castles of the fourteenth century still to be found in Britain, or on the continent of Europe, will afford many excellent hints for designing the external architecture of the main body, and especially of the appendages, of buildings in this style. For the arrangement of the interior, recourse must be had to the wants of modern society; for, as we have said before, the object, in cases of this sort, is never to mimic individual examples, but to imitate the general spirit of the style and manner."[73]

He showed smaller versions of such designs in the section on cottage dwellings, among them a battlemented house "for a man and his wife without children," also houses in "monastic Gothic," "castellated Gothic," and "the Elizabethan style." The latter, often vaguely called "old English," distorted and disguised the character of many buildings, large and small, in the Victorian period, for it was and is still favoured by speculative builders, and elaborated examples appeared in many later editions of the *Encyclopædia*. In the Supplement, prepared by Loudon and issued in the 1846 edition, three years after his death, a cottage was included "with ornamental elevations in the style of the ancient, half-timbered houses of England." This was described in detail, with practical suggestions for creating a genuine antique appearance. Thus the roof was to be "covered with thatch or reeds, in either case steeped in lime-water, and the chimney shafts to be of brick, to be splashed coarsely so as to imitate weather-stained bricks or stones."[74] Loudon observed that "Half-timbered cottages are very picturesque objects, and seem particularly appropriate to a woody country; nevertheless we cannot recommend them for general adoption, even if the expense were not an object, on account of the thinness of the walls, and the care requisite to keep the roof and other parts of the exterior in nice order."[75] Such considerations would not deter the speculative builder, and the craze for half-timbered buildings spread rapidly, and even affected railway architecture. Woburn station, on the Bedford branch of the London and Birmingham line, was described by Frederick S. Williams in *Our Iron Roads* as "the most picturesque with which the writer is acquainted. The tasteful arrangement of the building, and the contrast of the clean white walls with the oak framings, have, by the skill of the architect, combined to make it a decided ornament to a very beautiful neighbourhood."[76] The illustrations on page 56 suggest that the architect owed something to Loudon. All those labels, Gothic,

LOUDON'S COMMERCIAL GOTHIC

Above: Villa for a small family, in the "Castellated Style of Gothic Architecture." Loudon suggested that "the terrace walls, and other ornamental architectural appendages . . . should either be in some degree marked by the lines and finish of fortified walls, or should imitate their ruins." *Encyclopaedia,* Design XX, page 919.

Three suggestions for the style of a small cottage. *Above, left:* Castellated Gothic. *Right:* Monastic Gothic. *Below, right:* Elizabethan. *Encyclopaedia,* page 79.

Above, left: Cottage dwelling "for a man and his wife without children." Castellated Gothic is indicated. *Encyclopaedia,* page 67.

PUGIN'S COMMENT ON COMMERCIAL GOTHIC

"What can be more absurd than houses built in what is termed the castellated style?" said Pugin in *The True Principles of Pointed or Christian Architecture*, which was published in 1841, eight years after the first edition of Loudon's *Encyclopaedia*. In this illustration he parodied the absurdities of this make-believe style, and said: "all is a mere mask, and the whole building an ill-conceived lie."

Far more absurd than the "castellated style" was "Indian Gothic," adopted for this two-roomed dwelling. This "Indian cottage" was suggested as suitable for a childless country labourer and his wife. Loudon's *Encyclopaedia*, page 82.

LOUDON'S DESIGNS FOR DETACHED COTTAGES

Left: Single storey cottage, with four rooms, kitchen and back kitchen. *Encyclopaedia,* Design LV, page 187.

Right: Dwelling for a working man with a family. The style is "Old English." *Encyclopaedia,* Design XXV, page 96.

Left: Dwelling for a "Married couple and one child, with a Pigsty." In "the the old English manner." *Encyclopaedia,* Design X, page 49.

LOUDON'S DESIGNS FOR DOUBLE COTTAGES

Above: Two four-roomed dwellings under one roof. "We have engraved this design as it was sent to us," Loudon commented, "because, though it is full of faults, it contains the germs of great beauty and interest; and because it affords a very good example of the kind of impracticable designs which are frequently made by picturesque architects or amateurs." *Encyclopaedia,* Design LVII, pages 191–93.

Above: Two four-roomed cottages, which Loudon described as "comfortable, unobtrusive dwellings, expressive of nothing more than what they are." *Encyclopaedia,* Design LX, pages 194–97. *Below:* Two cottages for country labourers. Design XLVII, page 170.

The influence of Loudon's *Encyclopaedia* and *The Suburban Gardener and Villa Companion* is apparent in works like this station, at Woburn on the Bedford branch of the London and Birmingham railway. Included in *Our Iron Roads* (1852), and described by the author, Frederick S. Williams, as the most picturesque with which he was acquainted. It was, he said, "a decided ornament to a very beautiful neighbourhood" (pages 235–36). The half-timbered cottage with ornamental elevations shown below was included in the Supplement to the 1846 edition of Loudon's *Encyclopaedia*, and was designed by T. J. Ricauti (page 1147).

Elizabethan, Old English, had potent sales appeal: they were used freely by architects, builders, cabinet-makers, upholsterers, by every draughtsman or tradesman concerned with building and furnishing and decorating.

Such fashions, fostered by the Gothic revival, spread to the United States, where nearly every phase of Victorian taste had its counterpart in architecture, interior decoration and furniture design. In America, the Gothic and Greek revivals developed concurrently during the early years of the nineteenth

Old English cottage, formed of wooden framing, "raised on a cyclopian substructure." It was designed by William Wells and erected on his estate of Redleaf, in Kent. Included in Loudon's *The Suburban Gardener and Villa Companion* (1838), page 725, also in the Supplement to the 1846 edition of his *Encyclopaedia* as Design XXVIII, page 1171.

Thatched cottage, suitable for the superintendent of an estate. Reduced from Robinson's *Rural Architecture* (1829), and included in Loudon's *The Suburban Gardener and Villa Companion*, page 727

Left: Wood-built house in the Swiss style for a married couple and family. From Loudon's *Encyclopaedia*, page 46.

Right: Cottage dwelling in the German Swiss style. Stone or brick up to the first floor, wood construction above. From Loudon's *Encyclopaedia*, page 99.

Left: A gate lodge, combining a stable, in the Swiss style. From the Supplement to the 1846 edition of Loudon's *Encyclopaedia*, page 1148.

A villa in the Swiss style, designed by Edward Buckton Lamb (1806–69), for John Murray on a site near Stranraer. Included in the Supplement to the 1846 edition of Loudon's *Encyclopaedia*, Design I, page 1185.

century. A monumental, classical tradition survived until after the Civil War, that war between the States which accelerated the decline of so many American traditions; and in the 1840's it was seriously interrupted by such examples of Gothic design as Trinity Church in New York, built by Richard Upjohn, and Grace Church, by James Renwick. In 1841 Andrew Jackson Downing published his first book on building, entitled *Cottage Residences; or a Series of Designs for Rural Cottages and Cottage Villas, and their Gardens and Grounds adapted to North America*, and his most ambitious work, *The Architecture of Country Houses*, appeared in 1850. Both were lavishly illustrated with examples ranging from cottages in the "English or Rural Gothic style" to villas in the "Italian style, bracketed." The results have remained, and may be seen all over the Eastern States and the Middle West, incongruous intruders many of them, aliens in a countryside that had preserved, and still preserves, a traditional technique of frame house construction, based on the use of weatherboarding and double-hung sash windows, which has persisted since Colonial times.

Downing was entrusted with large commissions as a landscape gardener, and laid out the grounds of the Capitol, the Executive Mansion, and the Smithsonian Institute, at Washington, though the work was completed after his death, for he was drowned in a steamboat accident at the age of thirty-seven. Even in his short professional life, he acquired a great reputation, and wrote with confidence and authority, though he shared Loudon's tendency to explore

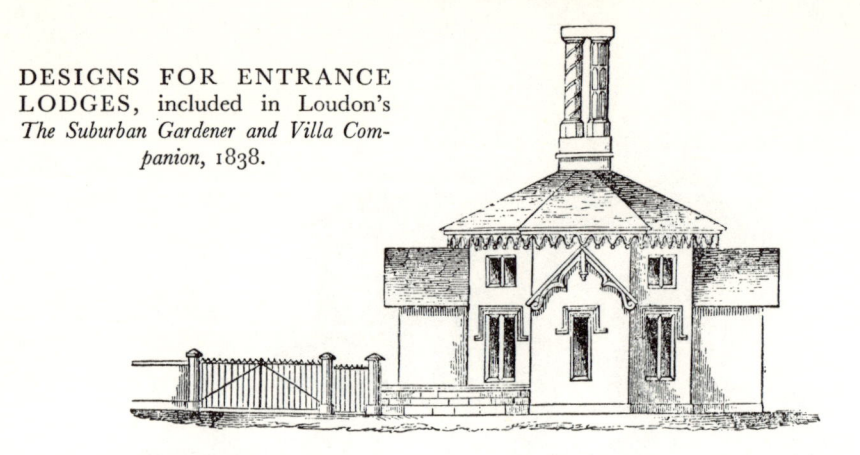

DESIGNS FOR ENTRANCE LODGES, included in Loudon's *The Suburban Gardener and Villa Companion*, 1838.

Above: Gothic entrance lodge, designed by Edward Brigden, page 724.

Left: Design for an entrance lodge to a villa. *Right:* A gate lodge in the Italian style. *Below:* Gate lodge in the Swiss style. These three designs were reduced from Robinson's *Rural Architecture* (1829) and included by Loudon in *The Suburban Gardener*, pages 727–28. (See pages 13 and 16.)

the perfectly obvious at inordinate length. "As all the satisfaction which the reason experiences in building as a useful art, arises from fitness, and expression of purpose," he wrote, "so all the delight which the imagination receives from architecture as an art of taste, is derived from *beauty of form*, and from the *sentiment* associated with certain modes of building long prevalent in any age or country."(77)

Like Washington Irving and many other American writers, he revered "the good old times," and fell for the "Merrie England" legend. "Not a little of the delight of beautiful buildings to a cultivated mind grows out of the *sentiment* of architecture, or the associations connected with certain styles," he said. "Thus the sight of an old English villa will call up in the mind of one familiar with the history of architecture, the times of the Tudors, or of 'Merrie England,' in the days of Elizabeth. The mingled quaintness, beauty, and picturesqueness of the exterior, no less than the oaken wainscot, curiously carved furniture and fixtures of the interior of such a dwelling, when harmoniously complete, seem to transport one back to a past age, the domestic habits, the hearty hospitality, the joyous old sports, and the romance and chivalry of which, invest it, in the dim retrospect, with a kind of golden glow, in which the shadowy lines of poetry and reality seem strangely interwoven and blended."(78)

That is pure Bracebridge Hall, in sentiment if not in style, and a sentence from *The Sketch Book* could follow on quite happily: "It was really delightful to see the old Squire seated in his hereditary elbow chair, by the hospitable fireside of his ancestors, and looking around him like the sun of a system, beaming warmth and gladness to every heart."(79) The spell of "Old England" affected Americans even more potently than the natives, and, like the Gothic revival, it was soon commercialised. Downing's description of "an irregular cottage, in the old English style" discloses how important he thought the superficial ornamental details were, while he never identified or even suspected the spirit of Gothic, as Pugin understood it. This particular design, shown on page 64, belonged "to that class of richly decorated, rural Gothic edifices, abounding in carved verge boards [the American equivalent of barge boards] and pendants, clustered chimney tops, and irregular outlines. There is something of grotesqueness, or at least fantastic richness in its details—something indicating a certain license of architectural imagination, not to be precisely measured by the standard of the rule and square, or the strictly utilitarian view."(80) His design for the small cottage or gate lodge, shown on page 65, would, he said, be the first thing to arrest the attention of a visitor, "and, with its old English, and pretty, rural expression, would serve as a prelude or agreeable preparation for the more varied and extensive cottage of the owner of the demesne."(81) As a gardener he believed that "Much of the pleasing effect of the most ornamental English cottages of this kind, arises from the employment of vines and other climbing plants of different sorts, which growing over and partly concealing portions of the exterior, render them, rich with blossoms, verdure, and fragrance, perfect wonders of rural beauty. For this purpose our Virginia creeper, the Trumpet monthly Honeysuckles, and the Boursalt, and English White Climbing Roses, are most suitable in this climate."[82]

Downing also advocated the "bracketed mode" for cottage villas, with a projecting roof, supported by decorative brackets, "so simple in construction, so striking in effect," and "highly suitable to North America, and especially to the southern states."[83] He thought that "a very ingenious architect might produce an *American cottage style*, by carefully studying the capabilities of this mode, so abounding in picturesqueness, and so easily executed." (See page 64.) The hint was taken by a good many architects and builders during the mid-nineteenth century, for the "bracketed" style became extremely popular: so did a lot of Downing's other suggestions, for his *Cottage Residences* and *The Architecture of Country Houses* were as celebrated as copy-books in America as Loudon's *Encyclopaedia* in Britain. He was alive to the absurdity of flimsy imitations, though he was oblivious to the enervating effect of imitation on the health of architectural design. "There is a glaring want of truthfulness sometimes practised in this country by ignorant builders, that deserves condemnation at all times," he declared. "This is seen in the attempt to express a style of architecture, which demands massiveness, weight and solidity, in a material that possesses none of these qualities. We could point to two or three of these imitations of Gothic castles, with towers and battlements built of wood. Nothing can well be more paltry and contemptible. The sugar castles of confectioners and pastry-cooks are far more admirable as works of art. If a man is ambitious of attracting attention by his house, and can only afford wood, let him (if he can content himself with nothing appropriate) build a gigantic wigwam of logs and bark, even a shingle palace, but not attempt mock battlements of pine boards, and strong towers of thin plank. The imposition attempted, is more than even the most uneducated person of native sense can possibly bear."[84] But it had already become an age of impostures and imitations, in architecture and all the arts and crafts and trades that served it, debilitated by the Battle of the Styles, and intoxicated by the name "antique," particularly when it was applied to furniture and such features of interior decoration as panelling and chimney-pieces.

The first English book on antique furniture, published in 1836, was Henry Shaw's *Specimens of Ancient Furniture*, with plates drawn and engraved from original examples, though some had been mutilated or enriched with inappropriate carvings of a later date, which was admitted by Sir Samuel Rush Meyrick who described the plates.[85] In 1838, Richard Bridgens published his designs for *Furniture with Candelabra and Interior Decoration*, with sixty plates of interiors and furniture in the Grecian and Elizabethan styles, and seven Gothic designs, some reproducing original articles.[86] It was a copy-book; there was no text: and many of the Elizabethan designs were clumsy, hybrid monsters.

DOWNING AND THE AMERICAN SCENE

Above: A suburban cottage, with a living-room, kitchen and bedroom on the ground floor and four bedrooms above. *Below:* An ornamental farmhouse, consisting of a hall, two bedrooms, a parlour and a pantry on the ground floor and a kitchen, dairy, wash-house and wood-house on the same level in an annex. Three bedrooms and a box room are on the floor above, and an attic in the roof. From *Cottage Residences*, by A. J. Downing (second edition, 1844). (See pages 64 and 65.)

DOWNING AND THE AMERICAN SCENE

Four more examples of designs from *Cottage Residences* are given on this page and opposite. *Above:* This is described as an "irregular cottage, in the old English style." *Below:* A cottage villa "in the Bracketed mode." (See page 63.)

DOWNING AND THE AMERICAN SCENE

Above: A villa in the Italian style, bracketed. "It is highly irregular," Downing wrote, "and while it will, on account of the greater picturesqueness and variety growing out of this circumstance, be more pleasing to a portion of our readers, a great number of persons, who only judge of a dwelling-house by a common-sense standard, will probably prefer a more regular and uniform building. . . ." *Below:* A small cottage or gate lodge, which would "make a neat and picturesque dwelling, if properly located, for a small, respectable family, who wish to lead a quiet and simple life." From *Cottage Residences*. (See pages 63 and 64.)

Interior of a bedroom in the Gothic style. From Downing's *The Architecture of Country Houses*, page 385, Fig. 181.

A receptive public existed for such things; an even larger public had acquired a taste for antiques, genuine and spurious; the undiscriminating collector appeared on the scene, and dealers in old furniture and junk increased and prospered.

How loot from the past was collected and arranged is recorded in Crofton Croker's book, *A Walk from London to Fulham*, which first appeared as a series of papers in *Fraser's Magazine*, and was edited and published by his son, Dillon Croker in 1860.[87] The last chapter describes a house "nestling in trees beneath the old tower of Fulham Church," called The Pryor's Bank, "which has been a pet kind of place of the Strawberry Hill class...." It was originally a humble, unpretentious dwelling, which was bought by a Mr. Walsh Porter, who "raised the building by an additional story, replaced its latticed casements by windows of coloured glass, and fitted the interior with grotesque embellishments and theatrical decorations. The entrance hall was called the robber's cave, for it was constructed of material made to look like large projecting rocks, with a winding staircase and mysterious in-and-out passages. One of the bedrooms was called, not inaptly, the lion's den. The dining-room represented, on a small scale, the ruins of Tintern Abbey; and here Mr. Porter had frequently the honour of receiving and entertaining George IV, when Prince of Wales. It was then called Vine Cottage, and having been disposed of by Mr. Porter, became, in 1813, the residence of Lady Hawarden; and, subsequently of

William Holmes, Esq., M.P., who sold it to Mr. Baylis and Mr. Lechmere Whitmore about 1834."

Both those gentlemen were romantic collectors; certainly not Gothic revivalists of the earnest type; and obviously had Horace Walpole's inclinations without his taste. "By them a luxurious vine which covered the exterior was cut down, and the cottage, named after it, replaced by a modern antique house. Mr. Baylis being a zealous antiquary, his good taste induced him to respect neglected things, when remarkable as works of art, and inspired him and his friend Mr. Whitmore with the wish to collect and preserve some of

Left: "An interior in the Bracketed style of a comparatively plain and simple kind, but showing its application to the ceiling, the windows, and the leading features of the apartment." *The Architecture of Country Houses,* Fig. 186, and pages 394–95.

Right: A parlour in a simple Gothic style, with a bay window at the end. From Downing's *The Architecture of Country Houses,* 1850, page 383, Fig. 178.

the many fine specimens of ancient manufacture that had found their way into this country from the Continent, as well as to rescue from destruction relics of Old England. In the monuments and carvings which had been removed from dilapidated churches, and in the furniture which had been turned out of the noble mansions of England—the 'Halls' and 'Old Places'—Mr. Baylis saw the tangible records of the history of his country; and, desirous of upholding such memorials, he gleaned a rich harvest from the lumber of brokers' shops, and saved from oblivion articles illustrative of various tastes and periods, that were daily in the course of macadamisation or of being consumed for firewood.

"The materials thus acquired were freely used by him in the construction of a new building upon the site of Vine Cottage, and adapted with considerable skill; but when neither the vine nor the cottage were in existence, it appeared to Mr. Baylis ridiculous to allow a misnomer to attach itself to the spot. After due deliberation, therefore, respecting the situation upon a delightful bank of gravel, and the association which an assemblage of ecclesiastic carvings and objects connected with 'monkish memories,' there collected, were likely to produce upon the mind, the new house was styled the 'Pryor's Bank.' "[88] An indiscriminate passion for collecting may destroy feeling for design and respect for fitness. The collectors who filled Pryor's Bank with Gothic odds and ends, were obviously delighted with the treatment of the dining-room, where "the greater portion of the Gothic oak panelling . . . originally formed the back of the stalls in the beautiful chapel of Magdalen College, Oxford. During the late repairs this panelling was removed and sold. Much of it was purchased by the Marquess of Salisbury for Hatfield House, and the remainder Mr. Baylis bought. More of the oak panelling in the room, especially the elaborately-wrought specimens and the rich tracery work, have been obtained from Canterbury Cathedral, York Minster, St. Mary's Coventry, and other churches."[89]

Those in charge of sacred edifices seem to have parted with their sense of responsibility: they certainly parted with many of their treasures, though perhaps more readily with Georgian than mediaeval woodwork, accepting instead the commercial Gothic supplied by popular architects, who restored churches with such drastic results that the word restoration became synonymous with destruction. After a vast amount of irreparable damage had been done by zealous architects, like Sir George Gilbert Scott, the Society for the Protection of Ancient Buildings was founded in 1877. This slowed down the process of spoilation, though nothing could stop it: the appetite for antique loot was well established among those who could afford to indulge it, while respect for age, or the appearance of it, had since the 1830's and 40's eroded critical awareness of design. The age of taste became a shadowy memory, and although the word *taste* was bandied about by architects and writers, it no longer meant adherence to known and accepted principles of design which provided standards for appraising good proportions, appropriate ornament and agreeable colour. Fashion was in control.

Sir Francis Meynell has described the distinction between taste and fashion, "so like, so profoundly unlike. Taste is personal, is idiosyncratic—the individual expresses and commits himself, nobody else. Fashion is the surrender of the individual to a committee. True your own taste may be the same as the taste of influential others, so that, between you, you may affect fashion. But Taste is individual; Fashion is an arbitration, or a compulsion and sometimes —sometimes—even a trade conspiracy."[90]

Both Loudon and Downing were guilelessly taking part in a trade and professional conspiracy, and helped Gothic to become a commercially successful fashion. They gave the public what it wanted, in Britain and America; their books were popular catalogues for the wares of architects, builders and tradesmen; and although a few discriminating people might suspect their authority, there could be no reservations about the rightness of the fashion for Gothic, especially after Ruskin had asserted that he had "no doubt that the only style proper for modern northern work, is the Northern Gothic of the thirteenth century. . . ."[91]

The residence of Andrew Jackson Downing, near Newburgh, New York: a survival of urbane, Georgian Gothic. (See plates 1 and 2.) Reproduced from Downing's *Treatise on the Theory and Practice of Landscape Gardening, adapted to North America.* (New York and London: Wiley and Putnam. Second edition, 1844.)

Interior of All Saints, Margaret Street, in the borough of St. Marylebone. Designed by William Butterfield, and built between 1849 and 1859. Externally the church was an example of Victorian "brutalism," and within, no space was left undecorated—frescoes, mosaics, variously tinted marbles and indifferent carving combined to create an effect of dazzling confusion. Reproduced from plate 19 of *The Old and New Churches of London*, by Alfred and J. M. Capes. London, 1880.

CHAPTER V

RUSKIN AND MORRIS

JOHN RUSKIN was born in 1819, the only son of a prosperous wine merchant. The characters of his parents, in particular of his mother, are revealed in his fragment of autobiography, *Praeterita*, where he describes the circumstances of his bleak, puritanical upbringing. In that joyless Evangelical household Ruskin's mind received indelible impressions that persisted throughout his life, and gave to his writings and public pronouncements a sacerdotal air. He was allowed no toys until he was five or six, and then only a cart and ball and two boxes of wooden bricks.[92] His mother, Margaret Ruskin, had decided, even before he was born, that her son was to go into the Church, and the story of his early childhood and the savage discipline imposed on him by this brutally religious woman, might have been invented by Dickens; but from the rigours of those early years he derived certain advantages. In later life he could say, "Nothing was ever promised me that was not given, nothing ever threatened me that was not inflicted, nothing ever told me that was not true." He knew where he was with those orderly limitations and routines, and was not unhappy; but the security of that moral environment encouraged the growth of earnest beliefs which, even in youth, developed into intractable certitudes, occasionally becoming identified with Divine authority.

His life was saddened by disappointing love affairs, innocent enough in the carnal sense, but deeply disturbing to his impressionable temperament. His unhappy marriage to Euphemia Gray, contracted in deference to his parents' wishes, lasted for five years; he was not in love with her and after the glamour of being married to a famous and wealthy man had faded, the neglected and unsatisfied girl must have found life insufferably dull. The annulment of the marriage, under Scots law—the wedding had taken place at Perth—was a great relief to both parties. Euphemia ultimately married Millais the painter, one of the romantic, adventurous Pre-Raphaelite Brotherhood, a tall, slim, intensely vital young man, ten years younger than Ruskin. Such exasperating and tragic personal affairs were kept in the background; they were not permitted to impinge on his life as a writer and critic; for he was a born writer, dedicated to the study of the fine arts and conscious of his mission as their interpreter. He travelled and wrote books and gave lectures on painting and architecture, made delicately precise drawings of architectural details and sculpture, and published his views on a variety of social and economic problems.

He began writing during childhood, and at nine was turning out verse in the manner of Pope. Literary success came early, and the first volume of *Modern Painters*, published when he was twenty-four, laid the foundations of a reputation that grew more and more impressive, until age and an assertive streak of self-righteousness impaired his faculties, and impelled him to resist and condemn new ideas. *The Seven Lamps of Architecture*, illustrated by his own careful drawings, appeared when he was thirty; the first volume of *The Stones of Venice* when he was thirty-two. His authority was then so great that he was able to change the course of public opinion about that brotherhood of young, innovating artists, the Pre-Raphaelites, who painted from nature with the utmost fidelity, and roused the fury of *The Times* and the rest of the Press, which condemned their work, largely because it was unlike anything that had been exhibited before at the Royal Academy. Although he regarded the name they had chosen as "unfortunate and somewhat ludicrous," Ruskin defended them in a letter to *The Times*, and wrote a pamphlet vindicating their approach to painting, though there was more in it about Turner and the general snobbish approach to art in the year 1851 than about the Pre-Raphaelite Brotherhood.

His influence as a writer and lecturer was astonishing, and his opinions on architectural taste and design gave a convincingly sacred character to the Gothic Revival, acceptable to the majority of religious people, who were repelled by the proselytising raptures of Pugin. It seemed so much more natural and proper for Ruskin to speak and write about God and to quote the Bible, than for Pugin to invoke the authority of the Church of Rome; also Ruskin was handsome—tall, slight and well dressed, while Pugin was podgy and frequently wore archaic, eccentric clothes. (See plates 4 and 5.) Ruskin became the trustworthy mentor, who could always be understood, whether he was indulging in passionate advocacy or royal indignation; there was no subtle catch in anything he might say, nothing Jesuitical, as there might well be in a pronouncement by Pugin, for the Victorians suffered from an almost pathological suspicion of Roman Catholics. Ruskin was accepted as a safe guide—inspiring, persuasive, and superlatively confident, and although he was preoccupied with the superficial aspects of architecture, his authority was seldom challenged. This preoccupation is disclosed in the preface to the second edition of *The Seven Lamps of Architecture*. "All high art," he wrote, "consists in the carving or painting natural objects, chiefly figures: it has always subject and meaning, never consisting solely in arrangement of lines, or even of colours. It always paints or carves something that it sees or believes in; nothing ideal or uncredited. For the most part, it paints and carves the men and things that are visible around it. And as soon as we possess a body of sculptors able, and willing, and having leave from the English public, to

St. James-the-Less, Thorndike Street, Vauxhall Bridge Road, Westminster, designed by George Edmund Street, and built 1860–61. The fresco above the chancel arch is by George Frederick Watts. The decoration is less opulent and the general effect less confusing than in Butterfield's church, on page 70, but the ornamental use of black and red bricks and squat granite columns exhibits Victorian disregard for colour and texture. From plate 33 of *The Old and New Churches of London*, by Alfred and J. M. Capes. London, 1880.

carve on the façades of our cathedrals portraits of the living bishops, deans, canons, and choristers, who are to minister in the said cathedrals; and on the façades of our public buildings, portraits of the men chiefly moving or acting in the same; and on our buildings, generally, the birds and flowers which are singing and budding in the fields around them—we shall have a school of English architecture. Not till then."

This was a moral approach to art, and Ruskin's words recall John Calvin's pronouncement, that "It remaineth therefore lawfull, that onely those things be painted and graven whereof our eyes are capable: but that the majesty of God which is farre above the sense of our eye, be not abused with uncomely devised shapes."(93)

Ruskin rejected all shapes as uncomely unless they were natural. They alone should supply the sculptor and painter with models, and in Gothic architecture natural forms were honoured, for it had been created by those artists, and he

St. Giles's, Camberwell, one of Sir George Gilbert Scott's first churches. In his *Personal and Professional Recollections* he gives this account of the work, which he did with his partner, Moffatt: "The old Church of St. Giles, Camberwell, was burnt down in 1840, and there was a public competition for designs for its re-erection. We competed, sending in a very ambitious design, groined throughout with terra-cotta. No one had an idea whose our plans were. The competition being close, we adhered scrupulously to its regulations. Mr. Blore acted as assessor, and reported in our favour. Tenders were received for our design, and came in, I think, pretty favourably, but a parish opposition being excited, and a poll called for, a compromise was at length made, and we were commissioned to prepare a less costly design, which resulted in the present structure." (Chapter II, page 92.) Reduced from plate 18, *The Old and New Churches of London*, by Alfred and J. M. Capes. London, 1880.

St. Mary's Church, Wimbledon, designed by Sir George Gilbert Scott and W. B. Moffatt and built in 1843. From *The History and Antiquities of the Parish of Wimbledon*, by William A. Bartlett. London: 1865.

believed "that the architect who was not a sculptor or a painter, was nothing better than a frame maker on a large scale." This he held to be a revealing truth, and once he had recognised its significance, "every question about architecture immediately settled itself without farther difficulty," and he saw "that the idea of an independent architectural profession was a mere modern fallacy. . . ."

Sculpture and painting were the only two fine arts possible to the human race. "What we call architecture is only the association of these in noble masses, or the placing of them in fit places," he said. "All architecture other than this is, in fact, mere *building*; and though it may sometimes be graceful, as in the groinings of an abbey roof; or sublime, as in the battlements of a border tower; there is, in such examples of it, no more exertion of the powers of high art, than in the gracefulness of a well-ordered chamber, or the nobleness of a well-built ship of war."

Such assertions, minimising the importance of architects, were acceptable to a public that was always ready to distrust the expert in matters of taste, and Gothic architecture which conferred such copious freedoms of form, encouraged the indulgence of purely personal fancies. His rejection of the classic orders and all they stood for has been quoted in Chapter I, and he set forth his case for the superiority of Gothic architecture under six headings in an appendix to his *Lectures on Architecture and Painting*, when they were published in book form. "1. That Gothic or Romanesque construction is nobler

The parish church of St. Mary Abbots, Kensington, rebuilt by Sir George Gilbert Scott, 1869–72. The spire is more ambitious in scale and decorative treatment than the earlier church of St. Matthias, Richmond, shown opposite. From plate 23 of *The Old and New Churches of London*, by Alfred and J. M. Capes. London, 1880.

St. Matthias, on Richmond Hill, Surrey, designed by Sir George Gilbert Scott. From a drawing published in *The Builder*, August 7th, 1858.

than Greek construction. 2. That ornamentation is the principal part of architecture. 3. That ornamentation should be visible. 4. That ornamentation should be natural. 5. That ornamentation should be thoughtful. 6. And that therefore Gothic ornamentation is nobler than Greek ornamentation, and Gothic architecture the only architecture which should now be built." In support of the second of these propositions, he repeated his conviction that "the highest nobility of a building does not consist in its being well built, but in its being nobly sculptured or painted."

The Renaissance he had condemned as a "foul torrent," dismissing the gracious classical rhythms it gave to buildings and streets with all the intolerance his Evangelical upbringing had fostered: such pleasurable and pagan harmonies were a denial of nature. Worse, they were suspiciously frivolous, and, of course, hopelessly limiting with their rules and set proportions for unifying vertical and horizontal elements. Unity was abominable. "Do not be afraid of incongruities," he urged his audience in the second of his *Lectures on Architecture and Painting*; "do not think of unities of effect. Introduce your Gothic line by line and stone by stone; never mind mixing it with your present architecture; your existing houses will be none the worse for having little bits of better work fitted to them; build a porch, or point a window, if you can do nothing else; and remember that it is the glory of Gothic architecture that it can do *anything*. Whatever you really seriously want, Gothic will do it for you; but it must be an *earnest* want."

Moral tone was thus to be imparted to what otherwise might merely minister to pleasure, though comfort was, significantly, included as an *earnest* want, for he continued his praise of Gothic in these words: "It is its pride to accommodate itself to your needs; and the one general law under which it acts is simply this—find out what will make you comfortable, build that in the strongest and boldest way, and then set your fancy free in the decoration of it. Don't do anything to imitate this cathedral or that, however beautiful. Do what is convenient; and if the form be a new one, so much the better; then set your mason's wits to work, to find out some new way of treating it. Only be steadily determined that, even if you cannot get the best Gothic, at least you will have no Greek; and in a few years' time—in less time than you could learn a new science or a new language thoroughly—the whole art of your native country will be reanimated."

In the first lecture he advised people who were building houses "to insist upon having the pure old Gothic porch, walled in on both sides, with its pointed arch entrance and gable roof above." Many took this advice, and their builders and architects often lifted something from Loudon's pages with regrettable results. He also drew attention to the charms of the bow window. "You surely must all of you feel and admit the delightfulness of a bow window," he said; "I can hardly fancy a room can be perfect without one. Now you have nothing to do but to resolve that every one of your principal rooms shall have a bow window, either large or small. Sustain the projection of it on a bracket, crown it above with a little peaked roof, and give a massy piece of stone sculpture to the pointed arch in each of its casements, and you will have as inexhaustible a source of quaint richness in your street architecture, as of additional comfort and delight in the interiors of your rooms."

He insisted that windows which did not project should have pointed arches, and countered the "futile and ridiculous" objection that they could not be fitted with "comfortable sashes," by saying: "I have lived for months in Gothic palaces, with pointed windows of the most complicated forms, fitted with modern sashes; and with the most perfect comfort. But granting that the objection were a true one—and I suppose it is true to just this extent, that it may cost some few shillings more per window in the first instance to set the fittings to a pointed arch than to a square one—there is not the smallest necessity for the *aperture* of the window being of the pointed shape. Make the uppermost or bearing arch pointed only, and make the top of the window square, filling the interval with a stone shield, and you may have a perfect school of architecture, not only consistent with, but eminently conducive to, every comfort of your daily life."

He found the melodious charm of mediaeval building terms irresistible. They had, he said, a "strange and thrilling interest...." For example: "Vault, Arch, Spire, Pinnacle, Battlement, Barbican, Porch, and myriads of such others, words everlastingly poetical and powerful whenever they occur...." He was overcome by such intoxicating vocables. What happened, he asked, if you removed from Scott's romances "the word and the idea *turret?* ... Suppose, for instance, when young Osbaldistone is leaving Osbaldistone Hall, instead of saying 'The old clock struck two from a *turret* adjoining my bed-chamber,' he had said, 'The old clock struck two from the landing at the top of the stairs,' what would become of the passage? And can you really suppose that what has no power over you in words has no power over you in reality? Do you think there is any group of words which would thus interest you, when the things expressed by them are uninteresting?"

He could see no promise in materials like cast- and wrought-iron that were being used in prefabricated units for such imaginative structures as the Crystal Palace; he thought it unlikely that iron and glass would "ever become important elements in architectural effort." In that first Edinburgh lecture he gave his reason for such a belief, and, referring to his audience as "a company of philosophers," said, "but you are not philosophers of the kind who suppose that the Bible is a superannuated book; neither are you of those who think the Bible is dishonoured by being referred to for judgment in small matters. The very divinity of the Book seems to me, on the contrary, to justify us in referring *every* thing to it, with respect to which any conclusion can be gathered from its pages. Assuming then that the Bible is neither superannuated now, nor ever likely to be so, it will follow that the illustrations which the

When the moral earnestness cooled off, the Gothic revival became an inspiration for stylistic tricks and trimmings, and, as Pugin observed in *The True Principles of Pointed or Christian Architecture* (1841): "many architects apply the details and minor features of the pointed style to classic *masses* and arrangements" with the sort of results seen *below*, where Gothic arches are pierced in a mass of brickwork surmounted by a balustrade that suggests a classic prototype. This illustration represents a small section of the carriageway fronting St. Pancras Station on the Euston Road, London, designed by Sir George Gilbert Scott. (See opposite page.) From "The Bane of English Architecture," by John T. Emmett, the fourth of his *Six Essays*, Unwin Brothers, London, 1891.

There is a distinct resemblance in the treatment of Gothic features in this part of St. Pancras Station, shown on the left, and the Fire Brigade Station at Richmond, Surrey, shown *above*. The fire station, designed by Richard Brewer, a Richmond architect, was built in 1870 on the site of the Watch-house or Lockup and the Stocks. (Reproduced from *Recollections of Richmond*, by Somers T. Gascoyne. Richmond, 1898.) The building is of red brick, trimmed with stone, with the sculptured heads of firemen in helmets and a bearded figure (possibly intended to be Father Thames, to whom Richmond was indebted for much of its prosperity, and the Fire Brigade for its water supply), ornamenting the façade above the double arches of the engine house. The building is no longer used as a fire station, and it was "*designed to be picturesque*, by sticking as many ins and outs, ups and downs, about it as possible." (Pugin. Both quotations are from page 62 of *The True Principles of Pointed or Christian Architecture*.)

The front of St. Pancras Station and Hotel, designed by Sir George Gilbert Scott, 1868–74. The illustration is reproduced, on a slightly reduced scale, from an engraving in *Old and New London*, Volume V, by Edward Walford, issued by Cassell, Petter and Galpin, 1872–78. It was described by Walford as "a most beautiful structure," and Scott himself said: "It is often spoken of to me as the finest building in London; my own belief is that it is possibly *too good* for its purpose, but having been disappointed, through Lord Palmerston, of my ardent hope of carrying out my style in the Government offices, and the subject having been in the meanwhile taken out of my hands by other architects, I was glad to be able to erect one building in that style in London." (*Personal and Professional Recollections*, by Sir George Gilbert Scott, edited by his son, G. Gilbert Scott. London: 1879. Chapter VII, pages 271–72.) The train shed, with its iron and glass vault with a span of 243 feet, was designed by W. H. Barlow, before Scott's design was conceived, and "as if by anticipation," said Scott, "its section was a pointed arch."

Bible employs are likely to be *clear and intelligible illustrations* to the end of time. I do not mean that every thing spoken of in the Bible histories must continue to endure for all time, but that the things which the Bible uses for illustration of eternal truths are likely to remain eternally intelligible illustrations. Now, I find that iron architecture is indeed spoken of in the Bible. You know how it is said to Jeremiah, 'Behold, I have made thee this day a defenced city, and an iron pillar, and brazen walls, against the whole land.' But I do not find that iron building is ever alluded to as likely to become *familiar* to the minds of men; but, on the contrary, that an architecture of carved stone is continually employed as a source of the most important illustrations. A simple instance must occur to all of you at once. The force of the image of the Corner Stone, as used throughout Scripture, would completely be lost, if the Christian and civilised world were ever extensively to employ any other material than earth and rock in their domestic buildings: I firmly believe that they never will; but that as the laws of beauty are more perfectly established, we shall be content still to build as our forefathers built, and still to receive the same great lessons which such building is calculated to convey...."

Such sentiments, indicative of mental immobility, could be taken seriously by a mid-Victorian audience, particularly a Scottish one; for the authority of the Bible was unshaken, and when Ruskin supported his views on building materials with a scriptural reference, Jeremiah i, 18, doubt would have amounted to blasphemy. Indeed to doubt Ruskin almost became a form of blasphemy, for "His strong belief in himself led him to conclude it to be the final proof of error and wrong-mindedness for another to differ from him." That was written in 1874, the year Ruskin refused the Gold Medal of the

The Royal Victoria Patriotic School, Trinity Road, Wandsworth Common, built in 1857 to the design of Rhode Hawkins. This rigid symmetrical composition lacks the robust vigour that Waterhouse gave to his reconstruction of Eaton Hall (see opposite page), though it possesses a cold dignity, partly derived from the pale grey brick and the slate roof used by the architect. It is now a training college. *Drawn by David Owen.*

View of Eaton Hall, Chester, from the lake. William Porden's Georgian Gothic structure was changed into this in the late 1860's and '70's. "The difficult task of reconstructing the huge palatial structure was entrusted in 1867 to Mr. A. Waterhouse, R.A., under whose superintendence Eaton, after thirteen years of ever-anxious thought, has been with exquisite taste developed into the present stately and magnificent palace. The style of the present building, which is of Manley stone, is early pointed Gothic, freely treated." The illustration and the quotation are from an article on Eaton Hall, by Rupert H. Morris, published in *The Graphic*, January 23rd, 1886, pages 93–100. Two interiors, showing Porden's original work, appear on plate 1.

Royal Institute of British Architects, in a contemporary assessment of his character and influence which appeared in *The Art Journal* in "Pen-Likenesses of Art-Critics." This belief was, the article continued, "as heroically as bluntly affirmed in unmistakable language in his earlier controversies, and we have seen nothing in his later writings to indicate any modification of this opinion. Acutely learned, subtilely dexterous of diction, magnificently rhetorical, intensely hostile to cants and deceptions of every species, penetrating the very marrow of aesthetic right and wrong by his moral chemistry; as fiercely prophetic of tongue as a maddened seer, implacable as a savage in his hates, yet tender-hearted and sympathetic as a maiden in his loves; illogical (yet we have read a letter of his to a distinguished poet in which he says, of himself, referring to a critical charge of this sort in one of the Reviews, if there be any one faculty which I possess above all others, it is the logical one), having no faculty of generalisation, always seeing things apart in minutest detail and from closest vision, the natural sight running to one extreme of material observation, and his imaginative sight to its opposite; as bitterly ingenious in fault-finding as eloquently extravagant in laudation and conclusion; the most sincerely impressible of theorists and fervid demolisher of false gods, with the loftiest ideas of man's duty and his own pet idealisms; vehemently publishing his intuitions and observations as immutable principles of life; rejoicing, like Job's war-horse in the battle, but easily made despondent; with an unbalanced brain, running to fine points and bent on Ruskinising the world—the while most inconsistently sad and angry because of failure—despite himself, John Ruskin has done much good work for us all in his adopted cause. He has stirred anew the languid currents of aesthetic thought both in England and America; incited a deeper interest and investigation into the motives as well as the methods of Art-education; suggested beautiful and noble ideas; disclosed fresh sources of enjoyment and inspiration; helped to reconcile Art with Nature, and put us in better fellowship with both; and, best of all, relentlessly exposed and denounced evils, driving to bay the mean parasites that habitually infest all good work and sound aims. In short, notwithstanding his many entanglements of thought, eccentricities of presentment, incapacity of putting objects and ideas relatively right, or of accurately measuring the differences between the little and the great, of seeing the world as it actually exists, of curbing his own egoism, unphilosophical turmoil of soul, foregone prejudices, constitutional irritability, restraining his passion for Utopias, and of making intellectual allowance for his own defective physical fibre—notwithstanding all these drawbacks, Ruskin has been a profitable as well as fascinating writer for the general reader."[94]

Through his writings and lectures, Ruskin indirectly determined the form and character of hundreds of buildings, though his ideas were frequently misinterpreted, for apart from cultivating earnestness it was not easy to know quite how to set about following his thunderous exhortations. Two buildings

The Law Courts in the Strand, the last large public building in the revived Gothic style. A competition was held in 1866, and twelve architects sent in designs, including Sir George Gilbert Scott, Edward Middleton Barry (1830–80), George Edmund Street (1824–81), and Alfred Waterhouse (1830–1905). Sir George Gilbert Scott observed in his *Personal and Professional Recollections* that the instructions for this competition "were unprecedented in voluminousness, and the arrangements were beyond all conception complicated and difficult, which was further enhanced by the insufficiency of the site." (Chapter VII, page 273.) The judging of the competition led to some involved and rather unjust manipulation of the marks, and ultimately the judges, who wanted to give the work to Barry, whose "architecture was approved by no one," according to Scott, "conceived the idea of linking on to him some other architect, in whose powers they had more confidence, and they pitched upon Mr. Street, whose arrangements no one had ever spoken in favour of." (Scott, *opus cit.*, pages 274–75.) Scott, although he was displeased at having wasted three-quarters of a year on the competition, said that the selection of Street was "as illogical and unfair a decision as could well have been come to; yet practically a good one, as it ensured a noble work: for an able and artistic architect can surely make a good plan, while no amount of skill in mere planning can by itself enable a man to produce a noble building." *Drawn by A. S. Cook.*

exist which were designed largely under his direction, the Oxford Museum and the Union Debating rooms (now the Library), both the work of a self-taught Irish architect named Benjamin Woodward (1815–61). The Museum, begun in 1855, was described by the architect as "Veronese Gothic," and as the work proceeded Woodward had to endure the constant interference of dons, who objected to the idea of leaving the external decoration to the whim of individual workmen, for a band of masons was employed to carve the Gothic ornaments that embellished the façade. He had, moreover, to endure the incessant advice of Ruskin, who had been instrumental in persuading the University authorities to choose a Gothic rather than a classic design. A lively account of these troubles is given in *The Tragedy of John Ruskin*, by Amabel Williams-Ellis, whose comment that between them, Ruskin and Woodward "produced, with infinite care, two buildings of unparalleled ugliness" is abundantly justified. "They appear to have been designed," she said, "by a man who had no sense either of colour or texture." Writing in 1928, she observed that "Even now, when three-quarters of a century must have mellowed them considerably, the steep roofs of purple slates relieved with patterns of green, and the large unpleasant bricks of one, and the gingerish stone of the other, are extremely grating."(95) These buildings were not the result of uninspired or unskilful interpretation of Ruskin's views on the glories of Gothic. As Mrs. Williams-Ellis points out, "In as far as a layman can direct a

St. Mark's, Battersea Rise, built 1873, by William White (1825–1900). A brick structure with an adventurous spire, obviously influenced by French and Flemish secular prototypes. The timber spire is covered by shingles. This deliberate attempt to create a picturesque composition is far less confused and haphazard than Richard Brewer's fire station at Richmond, built three years earlier. (See page 80.) White designed what is almost a duplicate of this church, also in Battersea: St. Mary-le-Park, Albert Bridge Road, built 1883. *Drawn by A. S. Cook.*

St. Columba, Kingsland Road, Shoreditch, by James Brooks, built 1867–71. A red-brick edifice in the heavy-handed picturesque style. From plate 21 of *The Old and New Churches of London*, by Alfred and J. M. Capes. London, 1880.

building ... Ruskin did direct and approve the Oxford Museum, and he still more approved the Union building. The truth is that they are only a very little, if at all, better than the average Victorian Gothic building which Ruskin rightly despised. It is necessary to bear these two buildings in mind if we feel inclined to yield sometimes in matters of architectural taste to Ruskin's sweet deluding tongue, and to his air of taste and erudition."[96]

Meanwhile, at Exeter College, an Oxford undergraduate named William Morris was reading Ruskin aloud to his circle of friends. "He had a mighty singing voice," according to J. W. Mackail, his biographer, "and chanted rather than read those weltering oceans of eloquence as they have never been given before or since. . . ."[97] Like Ruskin, Morris was the son of wealthy parents and was able to choose a way of life that gave the greatest scope for his gifts. He was born at Walthamstow in 1834, and was extremely delicate in his early childhood; perhaps because of this he learned to read at a very early age; certainly by the time he was four he had read most of the Waverley novels, and his life-long love of mediaeval civilisation may have arisen from Scott's picturesque misrepresentations. Indoctrinated from early childhood with the "Merrie England" legend, his love of literature was supplemented by an interest in architecture which he acquired in the three years he spent at Marlborough College, browsing in the school library, which was well supplied with books on the ecclesiastical branch of the subject, and on archaeology. Morris was just under fourteen when he entered Marlborough in 1848, and it was a very different sort of school from the Rugby that Dr. Thomas Arnold had created. It was opened in 1843, the year after Arnold's death, and though originally intended for the sons of clergymen, was unaffected by the stern sense of Christian duty which pervaded Rugby and was beginning to spread to other public schools, together with compulsory games and discipline conducted by pompous young specialists in tone and good form, variously dignified as prefects, praepostors or monitors. Marlborough in its early years enjoyed a comfortable chaos, which allowed great individual freedom. "There was no regular system of athletics. Cricket and football were only played by a small number of the boys. In play hours the bulk of them used to ramble about the country. There was no fixed school dress, and no prefect system."[98] There was no compulsion for a boy with strong individual tastes and exceptional abilities like Morris to conform to any conventional pattern. Marlborough in its early days of indifferent organisation was not dedicated, like other English public schools, to the mass production of reliable, insensitive athletic types, who would have cheered Old Brooke to the echo when he said: "I know I'd sooner win two School-house matches running than get the Balliol scholarship any day." A sentiment, incidentally, that would have displeased Dr. Arnold, as savouring of levity.[99] Morris left Marlborough, as he used to say afterwards, "a good archaeologist, and knowing most of what there was to be known about English Gothic."[100]

Columbia Market, Hackney, designed by Henry Astley Darbishire for the Baroness Burdett-Coutts, and built 1868–69. Describing the lofty Gothic hall, illustrated above, which was the chief feature of the building, Edward Walford said: "The exterior of this edifice is particularly rich in ornamentation. The basement is lighted by a range of small pointed windows, above which is an ornamental string-course. The hall itself, which is reached by a short flight of steps, is lighted by seven large pointed windows on each side, with others still larger at either end; the buttresses between the windows terminate in elaborate pinnacles; in fact, the whole building, including the louvre in the centre of the roof, and the tall clock-tower, bristles with crocketed pinnacles and foliated finials. Whether the building is too ornate, or whatever may be the cause, it is not for us to say; but, at all events, as a place of business in the way designed by its noble founder, Columbia Market from the very first has proved a comparative failure." (*Old and New London*, Volume V, by Edward Walford. London: Cassell, Petter and Galpin, 1872–78. Chapter XL, pages 505–6.)

Apparently he acquired only a sketchy knowledge of other subjects, and at Christmas 1851 his school life ended, and was followed by a year with a private tutor. He matriculated at Exeter College, Oxford, in June, 1852, but the college was full, and he did not go into residence until the following January.

He went up to Oxford with the intention of taking holy orders, and there he met some exceptional young men: Burne-Jones, also a freshman, with whom he became acquainted during the first days of their first term, and a little colony at Pembroke, from King Edward's School at Birmingham, which included Fulford, Henry Macdonald, and Cormell Price, who became the headmaster of the United Services College at Westward Ho, Bideford, where Kipling went to school. Kipling's portrait of Price, who is called Bates in *Stalky & Co.*, is oddly misleading, but there is one sentence which recalls the optimistic vitality of the group at Oxford. It occurs in the story called "The Last Term," and follows a description of the Head in his library, talking to Beetle who was editing the school paper, and reading verses from English poets aloud to the receptive boy. "And, slow breathing, with half-shut eyes above his cigar, would he speak of great men living, and journals, long dead, founded in their riotous youth; of years when all the planets were little new-lit stars trying to find their places in the uncaring void, and he, the Head, knew them as young men know one another."(101)

That group of young men was known as "The Brotherhood," and they discussed everything under the sun, and their interests ranged from theology and ecclesiastical history to art and architecture. Burne-Jones, like Morris, had intended to go into the Church, but both abandoned that ambition, as they came to realise that their desire to improve social conditions could be fulfilled by using their own special gifts: the priesthood was altogether too limiting for a man of such versatility as Morris, and he decided to become an architect, and in 1856 entered the office of George Edmund Street as a pupil. That enthusiasm did not last, and he abandoned his career as an architect because he soon realised that the arts and crafts were unfree in the industrial age, where the architect was a professional man who dictated everything from his drawing-board and left nothing to the skill or discretion or inventiveness of the individual workman. The joy had departed from work; the common arts and crafts of England were passing away; soon they would merely be interesting survivals. The conditions that had caused such a state of affairs were detestable, and his passionate protest against them led him, logically enough, to embrace socialism; but a picturesque, artistic socialism, which was to restore pride in work and re-establish the crafts that were threatened with extinction by machinery. He acknowledged Ruskin as the master-rebel who had inspired him, and in one of his last essays, written in 1894, said ". . . how deadly dull the world would have been twenty years ago but for Ruskin! It was through him that I learned to give form to my discontent, which I must say was not by any means vague. Apart from the

This pulpit was described as "professional 'religious art' at Westminster," by John T. Emmett in his essay on "Religious Art," in *The British Quarterly Review*, October 1st, 1875. (Included in his *Six Essays*, issued in book form in 1891.) In criticising the design he said: "The pulpit proper ought, of course, to be the subject of the highest workmanship and art, but here a meagre shell, on which a few crude panels set up lozengewise are introduced to give some childish notion of original design, is the true pulpit, and the incongruous details, which give painful emphasis to its impoverishment, are only adjuncts. Then, the lozenges are filled, to order, with inferior mosaic work, in one compartment with a poor ill-looking face, surrounded by the tradesman's ignorant suggestion of a wreath of thorns. . . ."

desire to produce beautiful things, the leading passion of my life has been and is hatred of modern civilisation."(102)

He wrote bitterly of the "eyeless vulgarity which has destroyed art, the one certain solace of labour," and in summing up his reasons for becoming a socialist said that "the study of history and the love and practice of art forced me into a hatred of the civilisation which, if things were to stop as they are, would turn history into inconsequent nonsense, and make art a collection of the curiosities of the past, which would have no serious relation to the life of the present." In *News from Nowhere*, he described a socialist utopia which had repudiated industrialism, reinstated handicrafts, and in architecture had picked up the threads of the pre-Renaissance English tradition. It was the "Merrie England" legend, given the substance of a great creative artist's knowledge of architecture and the crafts; a utopia in which Gothic was no longer the product of an artificial revival but the work of people who had recognised its capacity for fresh development. *News from Nowhere* first appeared

Bookcase and writing table of oak, designed by Norman Shaw and executed by James Forsyth, the sculptor. It was included in the International Exhibition of 1862. The designer was obviously thinking in terms of brick and stone; the properties and character of wood are ignored, and an architectural composition, conceived on a drawing-board, is masquerading as a piece of furniture. Those budding tourelles on the upper part are a hint of shapes to come. (See New Scotland Yard on plate 9.)

The influence of Ruskin's confused counsel is as obvious in this early example of Shaw's work—he was only thirty-one when he designed it—as in the houses put up by speculative builders in the 70's and 80's, of the kind shown below, with their panels of ornamental brickwork and frills of Gothic ornament. These terrace houses are on the east side of Vardens Road, Battersea. (See plate 6 for the earlier west side development of this road.) *Drawn by A. S. Cook.*

in instalments during 1890 in *The Commonweal*, the organ of the Socialist League, which Morris had founded and edited. A year earlier, in a lecture to the Arts and Crafts Exhibition Society, he had said: "Art cannot be dead so long as we feel the lack of it . . . and though we shall probably try many roundabout ways for filling up the lack; yet we shall at last be driven into the one right way of concluding that in spite of all risks, and all losses, unhappy and slavish work must come to an end. In that day we shall take Gothic Architecture by the hand, and know it for what it was and what it is."

Morris possessed "the architectural instinct, the faculty of design in its highest form,"[103] and this is apparent in his work as an executant craftsman, in the pattern of his poems, in the supple rhythm of his prose. Although he rejected contemporary civilisation, and urged people to forget its pretentious architectural follies and careless waste and dirt and muddle, he was aware of the latent promise of industry; he could see the factory as it might be, with buildings "beautiful with their own beauty of simplicity as workshops, not bedizened with tomfoolery as some are now, which do not any the more for that hide their repulsiveness,"[104] and his dislike of machines was no recrudescence of the Luddite spirit, for he believed that "in a true society these miracles of ingenuity would be for the first time used for minimising the amount of time spent in unattractive labour, which by their means might be so reduced as to be but a very light burden on each individual."[105] But he never pursued such prophetic visions; in the late nineteenth century they were perhaps too remote from actuality, so instead he urged forgetfulness of existing chaos.

> "Forget six counties overhung with smoke,
> Forget the snorting steam and piston stroke,
> Forget the spreading of the hideous town;
> Think rather of the pack-horse on the down,
> And dream of London, small, and white, and clean,
> The clear Thames bordered by its gardens green. . . ."[106]

As Professor Pevsner has observed, there is a "decisive antagonism" in the life and teaching of Morris. "His work, the revival of handicraft, is constructive; the essence of his teaching is destructive."[107] From its inception, the handicraft revival was tinged with romantic antiquarianism. The mediaeval past afforded a refuge from the clamorous realities of prosperous Victorian industrialism. Morris edited that past, ran a mental blue pencil through its miseries and limitations and intolerable suffering, so that the English Middle Ages took on the likeness of an illuminated manuscript, unsoiled by ugly facts, aglow with brilliant colours, and packed with inspiring texts and examples. He wanted to see houses and cities growing into beauty under the hands of craftsmen; he wanted wood and stone to be carved freely

Sideboard designed by Philip Webb (1831–1915) and made by Morris and Company. Described as a "small buffet" it was 5 feet long and 1 foot 4 inches deep. From *Decoration and Furniture of Town Houses*, by Robert W. Edis, page 112. This is an obvious progenitor of the work of Ernest Gimson, Sidney Barnsley and Ambrose Heal, and of the earlier designs of Gordon Russell. It has affinities with the simple furniture made by mid-seventeenth-century Puritan craftsmen.

and surfaces to carry a burning splendour of decoration; and to this end he mastered a number of crafts himself.[108] To Morris and to many other artists and designers industry was regarded as a cancerous growth, and if it could not be cut out of civilisation then some part of the social body must be kept sweet and healthy by recalling the conditions of the past, and by dreaming of sunny utopias in which no wheel was turned save by the breeze or running water or the power of living muscle.

The house that Philip Webb built for him at Upton, in Kent, was the forerunner of a revival in domestic architecture, which supplied the framework of the handicraft revival. It was called the Red House, built on an L-shaped plan, with two stories, walls of red brick and a high-pitched red-tiled roof. For some undisclosed reason the sitting-rooms, dining-room, drawing-room, and hall all faced north. It was comfortably independent of any style: the oriel windows and gables were unostentatiously romantic, possessing the "quaint richness" that Ruskin had applauded, and it was a sincere attempt on the part of some gifted people to solve an architectural problem without reference to any prototypes. (Plate 7.)

Morris and those who shared his sympathies felt that architecture should arise naturally and joyfully from a revival of the crafts, and that the work of a brotherhood of craftsmen must transcend the tyrannical harmonies imposed by the Renaissance. Morris tried to resurrect the creative spirit of the men who had made the mediaeval abbeys and guild halls, and after the building of the Red House, he discovered that every branch of decorative and applied art in England was in a state of advanced decay. It was impossible to buy well-designed furniture, fabrics, or wallpapers, and in order to elevate standards of domestic design, the firm of Morris and Company was founded in 1861. Philip Webb, Burne-Jones, Rossetti, Ford Madox Brown, Faulkner and Marshall were associated with Morris in this venture, and the firm was prepared to undertake church decoration, carving, metalwork, stained glass, and also to design wallpaper, chintzes, carpets and furniture.

While handicrafts could be revived, or their extinction delayed, those who practised them could not exist on the joy of work alone; so Morris perforce found himself working for the relatively tiny section of the community that had both riches and artistic perception. The lives and homes of the common people were untouched, and common art was not restored to ordinary, everyday life. Presently the costly products of organised handicraft were imitated by industry. Morris had, quite unintentionally, started a vogue for "handmade" articles, so manufacturers had a new sales story for their wares. The machine was equal to the demand for "art" products; and the handicraft note was simulated by speckling metalwork with mock hammer marks and leaving woodwork rough and heavy. Where no external evidence of handwork could be faked, "quaintness" of form or ornament was emphasised.

Some handicrafts had been precariously preserved through the influence of Morris; but in providing opportunities for a few craftsmen to work, he had omitted to provide them with the right customers. It was galling for their activities to be supported by the "arty" rich, while the "people" were hungry for colour and gaiety and carving and folk songs amid the reek of the factory chimneys and the noise of machinery. The enthusiastic supporters of the handicraft revival had what in modern advertising is called a "brand image" of the English people, based largely on biased observation of a few rural types, though Morris knew that there were people who worked so hard "that they may be said to do nothing else than work, and are accordingly called 'the working classes,' as distinguished from the middle classes and the rich, or aristocracy. . . ."[109] Morris had his own "brand image" of the singing, dedicated craftsman, a figure almost as remote and improbable as the Golden Dustman in *News from Nowhere*.[110] Both misty images arose from the "Merrie England" legend. Meanwhile his work and teaching gave fresh impetus to romantic antiquarian taste, established an exaggerated reverence for handwork and handicraftsmen, indirectly encouraged blind admiration of the antique, which begot the curse of sterile imitativeness, atrophied critical judgment of design, and, by sanctioning the intolerance of the creative artist for machinery, robbed industry of immeasurable advantages, by making him a stranger to businesses where he should most properly have been a partner, thus delaying for over half a century the emergence and recognition of the industrial designer.

A contemporary misrepresentation of the teachings and ideas of William Morris, shown at the International Exhibition, 1872. Reproduced from the illustrated supplement on the Exhibition published in Volume XI of *The Art Journal*, page 29, this exhibit shows "the End of a Room, consisting of a stone and marble fireplace inlaid with hand-painted tiles, representing birds, foliage, and subjects—'The Song,' and 'The Tale,' 'The Jest' and 'The Book.' Carved oak framing, with mirrors and painted panels; the subjects—'Work' and 'Play.' Carved and decorated cornice; subjects—'Maternal Affection,' 'Conjugal Affection,' and 'Filial Affection.' Also a Canterbury and music-stand combined, of carved oak and novel construction, and a Flower-stand with painted tiles and brass lamp." (See page 99.)

Like Ruskin, Morris rejected the Renaissance, seeing it as the beginning of that separation of art from everyday life which had dislocated the patronage, practice and enjoyment of architecture and the crafts in England since the sixteenth century. He found it difficult to put himself in the frame of mind which could accept such a work as St. Paul's Cathedral "as a substitute for even the latest and worst Gothic building."[111] Neither St. Paul's in London nor St. Peter's in Rome were "built to be beautiful, or to be beautiful and convenient," he said. "They were not built to be homes of the citizens in their moments of exaltation, their supreme grief or supreme hope, but to be proper, respectable, and therefore to show the due amount of cultivation, and knowledge of the only peoples and times that in the minds of their ignorant builders were not ignorant barbarians. They were built to be the homes of a decent unenthusiastic ecclesiasticism, of those whom we sometimes call Dons now-a-days. Beauty and romance were outside the aspirations of their builders."[112]

Buildings like the St. Pancras Hotel, by Sir George Gilbert Scott, with its repellent texture and congested mixture of French and Venetian Gothic details, were thus presumed to be superior to Wren's great church. (See page 81.) The demands of a religious architectural revival limited the few good architects of the period, and there was a shortage of good architects, though there were plenty of men whose energy and commercial acumen enabled them to build up vast practices. At the height of his career, Scott had more jobs in hand than he could possibly remember, and on one occasion when he left London by an early morning train, he telegraphed to his office from a station in the Midlands, asking: "Why am I here?" The story, often told, is probably true: and it illustrates the fabulous activity of a successful Victorian architect.[113] Scott gloried in Gothic, though rather than lose the commission for the Government offices in Whitehall, for which he had competed successfully, he changed his winning composition of mullioned windows, gables and steep-pitched roofs for a Renaissance design, when Lord Palmerston, the Prime Minister, refused to tolerate anything except a classic building. It was a major defeat for the Gothic side in the Battle of the Styles, but Scott had many victories to console him, and distributed his pious enthusiasms throughout the land. George Edmund Street, Scott's pupil and Morris's first master, who built the Law Courts in the Strand and a great number of churches, shared his mentor's outlook, and the work of both men revealed the narrow vision and the drawing-board approach of the commercially successful Gothic revivalists. In the confident vulgarity of such work as the Albert Memorial, completed in 1872, Scott showed how design was wholly subordinated to ornament, which had become, as Ruskin had said it should become, the principal part of architecture. (Plate 3.) Even though this was widely accepted by architects, Morris's tranquil dreams of craftsmen enriching buildings joyfully and spontaneously remained unrealised. As a result of the Gothic Revival, there was a demand for masons and carvers who were able to reproduce mediaeval forms of ornament; but such men were very rare, though, as mentioned in Chapter III, a few did exist in small family building businesses in remote rural districts. Craftsmen were not only diminishing in numbers, but in the uncongenial industrial environment of the Victorian age their economic and social status was doubtful, and even the amateur craftsman was hardly respectable. Could a craftsman, a man who thought and worked with his hands, ever be accorded the respect that a clerk could claim? Could a well-to-do father regard, save with dismay, his son's decision to become a mason, a cabinet-maker, or a smith? It was trying enough for a Victorian parent when a son announced his intention of taking up painting, or music, or writing; although such creative activities occasionally redeemed their disrepute by proving lucrative. Even so, the rewards were uncertain, and the life morally loose and unwholesome, unregulated by proper office hours.

Of course, men of the stature and social position of Morris were exempt from such critical doubts; but a good many people began to be uneasy about his socialistic activities. In every generation an overdose of vitality is poured into a chosen few, thus making nonsense of the doctrine of equality; but the human receptacles are often the most passionate advocates for equalitarian systems; and Morris was one of them. Many of his perplexities were resolved by his conversion to the simple socialism of the '80's and '90's, which bore about the same relationship to modern Marxism as Georgian romantic Gothic did to the Christian Gothic of the Revival. The social revolution, which seemed so promising and so near, was beginning to spend its force in battles concerned with scales of payment and conditions of work, rather than with the work itself, though to be sure the objective was "a fair day's pay for a fair day's work," for restrictive practices and "working to rule" had not been thought of, and would indeed have seemed idiotic and sinful nonsense to Morris and all his genteel fellow socialists. They were the only people who ever mentioned the finest reward for all work, which is true pride in it.

One practical expression of Morris's ideas and beliefs, apart from the handicraft revival, influenced the trend of architectural design: the Red House which Philip Webb had built for him became the progenitor of a new school of domestic architecture. It possessed an emotional appeal; it had a romantic originality, and the architect's skilful use of red brick and tiles led to the rediscovery of texture. It encouraged many architects to make experiments in comfortable associations of materials, embodied in attractive features, gables, porches and bays, not diligent reproductions of mediaeval models or copied from carefully filed drawings of Gothic detail, but homely and spontaneous, as though the native English tradition in design had been continued from the point where it had been interrupted in the mid-sixteenth century. The colour and texture of materials became more important than ornament.

A cabinet in the mediaeval style, made by Collier and Plucknett of Warwick for the Rev. W. K. W. Chafy Chafy, and shown at the International Exhibition of 1872. The cabinet was of oak, the columns of solid ebony, with light oak capitals, the surface inlaid with various woods, and the shelves edged with a border of purple velvet, embroidered with gold. This cabinet suffers from the same ineffectual muddling with architectural features that mars Norman Shaw's bookcase and writing table shown on page 92. Reproduced from the illustrated supplement on the Exhibition in Volume XI of *The Art Journal*, page 24.

Half-timbered construction, with rough plaster or brick set in herringbone patterns, between oak uprights, could produce agreeable effects. Roofs could press down their warm load of red tiles almost to the ground in places, for the roof flowed over and down the walls, while a thrusting family of dormers emerged through it, spiked with decorative finials. Speculative builders produced their own repellent variations, and continued to build "old world" and "off-Tudor" houses and bungalows for the next fifty years.

The teachings and work of Morris were taken far more seriously in Europe than in England, and the Scandinavian countries profited greatly by applying his ideas and thereby smoothing the transition from handicrafts to machine production. One of the great architectural results of his teaching is Ragnar Östberg's Town Hall at Stockholm, perhaps the last romantic building to be erected in Europe, before romance was supplanted by modernism. But, as Pevsner has pointed out, Morris was "the true prophet of the twentieth century, the father of the Modern Movement. We owe it to him that an ordinary man's dwelling-house has once more become a worthy object of the architect's thought, and a chair, a wallpaper, or a vase a worthy object of the artist's imagination."[114]

Morris was a robust lover of life, as ebullient and indignant as Dickens, and, at times, as angry as Pugin; but his work as a craftsman and a writer sweetened his life with a sense of personal fulfilment; he was an intelligent artist, and his protests against the evils and abuses of his time are free from the peevish, falsetto notes of Ruskin, nor is there any hint of the thin red whine of the latter-day intellectual. Both Ruskin and Morris helped to change the environment of Victorian life, but because their ideas were often interpreted by lesser men, and indeed by people who had no interest in art or architecture or anything apart from commercial gain, they contributed a great deal of confusion to the Victorian scene. But it would have been less lively and unexpected and grotesque without them, and might possibly have been even duller and uglier.

CHAPTER VI

THE CLASSIC TRADITION AND THE UNRECOGNISED STYLE

SUPERFICIALLY, the architectural background of the Victorian scene might appear to be triumphantly Gothic, while classic was discredited and deliberately played down, or, at the best, condoned for some special, or specious, reason. When Lord Palmerston compelled Scott to use a classic design for the Foreign Office building, the most elaborate arguments were advanced by his admirers to prove that only a master of Gothic architecture could produce a great classic building. *The Art Journal* published an article on the controversy the building had provoked and after some exultant praise, said: "Unconsciously Lord Palmerston adopted exactly the right course of action to secure the most perfect expression of classic Art, when he required a classic design to be produced by an experienced Gothic architect, for the Gothic is such admirable Architecture, that a master of Gothic Art is *ipso facto* a master of architecture, and therefore he is pre-eminently qualified to deal as well with the classic as with the Gothic Style. Mr. Scott's training and experience as a Gothic Architect, instead of raising up an insurmountable barrier between himself and classic Art, were of far greater value to him than any other possible training and experience, when he sat down to produce his first great classic design; and throughout the subsequent progress of the work their supreme value has been demonstrated in the most impressive manner. And thus, reversing the specious, but not very profound, *dictum*, that a successful modern classic building must necessarily be designed and erected by a classic architect of mature experience, the signal success of the new Foreign Office has mainly resulted from the fact that the architect is the most experienced living master of the Gothic, as he certainly is one of the most consistent as well as devoted admirers and lovers of that style of Art."[115]

But a classic tradition persisted until the end of the period, and was expressed with copious variations by architects, who were not exhibiting a reluctant ambidexterity like Scott, but used the Greek and Roman orders because they has taken the classic side in the Battle of the Styles. The results differed in character from the buildings of the late seventeenth and eighteenth centuries as obviously as Victorian clothes differed from Georgian. The classic tradition

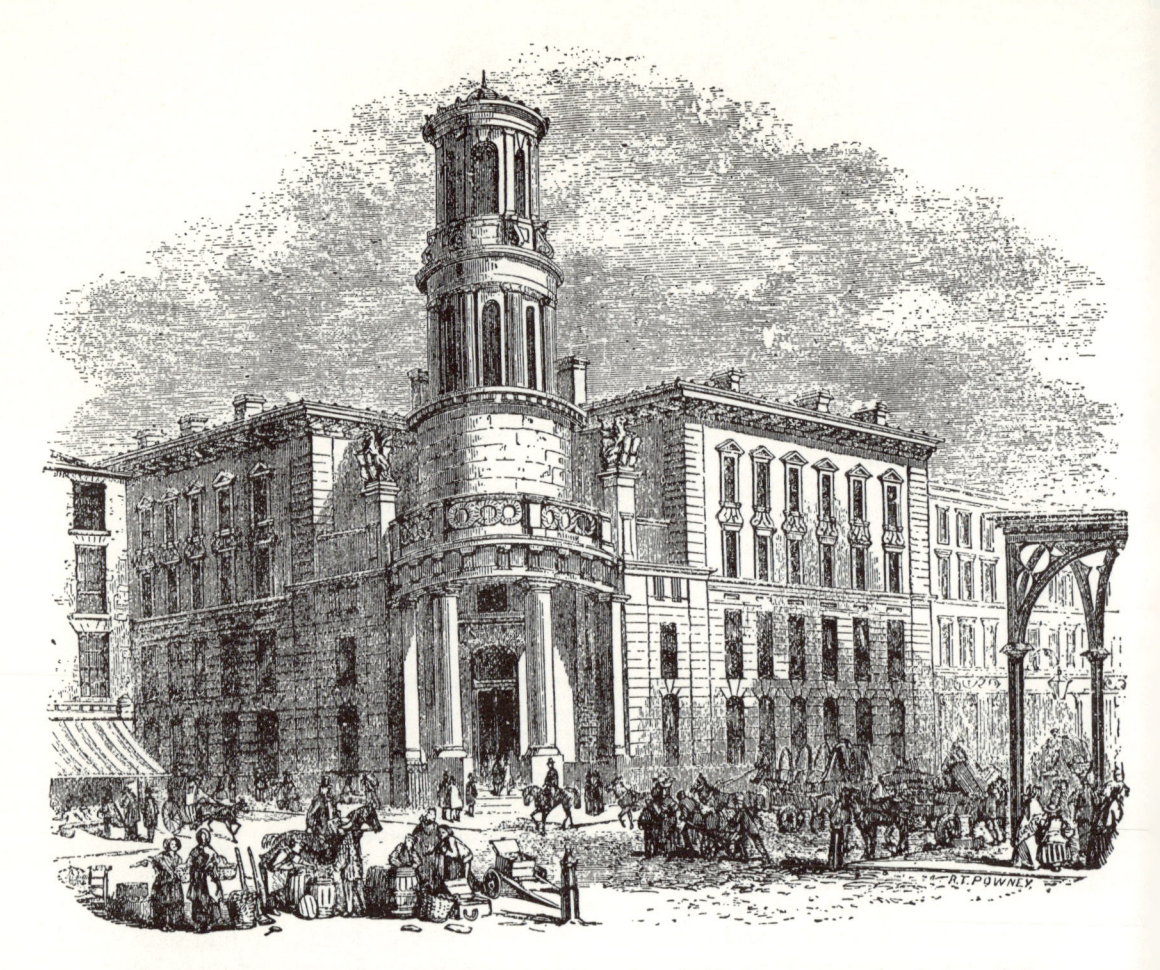

The Coal Exchange, Lower Thames Street, London, built 1847–49, to the design of the City Corporation's architect, James Bunstone Bunning (1802–63). A bold and original composition, though beginning to suggest a heavy-handed use of the classic idiom that was to give corpulence and clumsiness to so many mid- and late-Victorian buildings. The exterior conveys no hint of the inventive use of industrial materials, cast-iron and glass, in the Rotunda behind the masonry façade. Reproduced from an engraving in *Old and New London*, Volume II, edited by Walter Thornbury and issued by Cassell, Petter & Galpin, 1872–78. (See plate 20.)

ceased to be an inspiration after the Greek Revival; it froze into a convention, imposing an air of palsied respectability on all kinds of buildings. During the last decades of the Victorian age, it was regurgitated by architects like Norman Shaw who produced a so-called Queen Anne Revival in the 1870's and '80's, while in the United States a far more scholarly and correct resumption of classic design was marked by the work of McKim, Mead and White. That famous partnership gave new life to the Colonial tradition and refreshed the tired spirit of the Renaissance. "No architects ever turned Colonial motifs to so good an account," wrote Sir Charles Reilly, "enlarging and reinforcing them until such architecture grew in their hands into a style suited to town buildings as well as to country ones, to large ones as well as to small."[116] Although the Colonial tradition in America had to compete with the lavish confusion of styles popularised by Downing and his contemporaries, that tradition was never superseded and still survives. No comparable survival of the classic idiom linked British domestic architecture with the Georgian period, though the urban development of London and other cities included many tall stuccoed terraces with the solemn Doric or Ionic columned porticoes that Ruskin had jeered at when he said: "You know how the east winds blow through those unlucky couples of pillars. . . ." Villages like Battersea and Putney were becoming respectable middle-class suburbs, reflecting on a smaller

Osborne House, the Royal residence in the Isle of Wight, designed by Thomas Cubitt (1788–1855) in collaboration with Prince Albert. Reproduced from *Leaves from the Journal of Our Life in the Highlands, from 1848 to 1861*, by Queen Victoria, page 106.

scale the dignity of South Kensington. Such versions of the classic tradition were often derived from Loudon, and some of the terraces and semi-detached houses built during the '60's and '70's might have been reproduced unaltered from his *Encyclopaedia*. (The west side of Vardens Road, Battersea, shown on plate 6 is typical of such suburban development.)

There were Italianate buildings, as varied in composition and detail as Osborne House, the Royal residence in the Isle of Wight, designed by Thomas Cubitt in collaboration with Prince Albert, or St. Thomas's Hospital on the Lambeth bank of the Thames, facing the Houses of Parliament, designed by Henry Currey. (See page 103 and below.) The Imperial Institute at South Kensington, by Thomas Edward Colcutt, with its ponderous fussiness and pretentious amalgam of French early Rennaissance motifs, illustrates the Victorian love not only of lavish ornament but of towers for their own sake. (See plate 11.) Ruskin had said that from the days of the Tower of Babel, "whenever men have become skilful architects at all, there has been a tendency in them to build high; not in any religious feeling, but in mere exuberance of

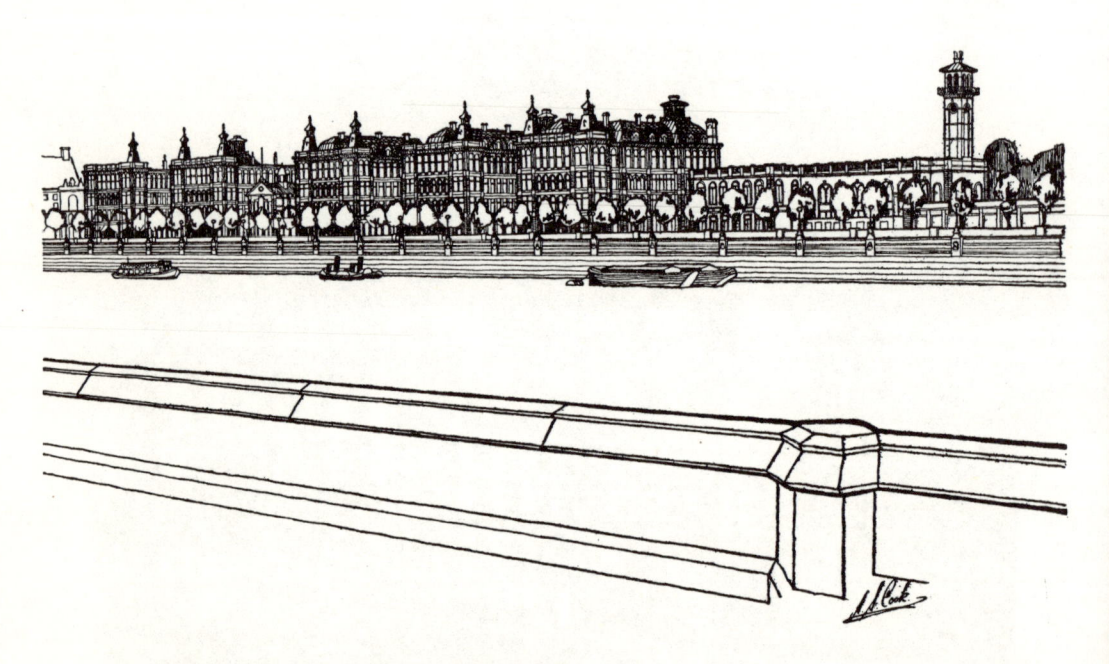

St. Thomas's Hospital, on the south bank of the Thames, between Lambeth Palace and Westminster Bridge, and opposite the Houses of Parliament. Designed by Henry Currey (1820–1900), and built between 1868 and 1871, it was an example of Italianate Victorian drawing-board architecture. Criticising the design, John T. Emmett said: "Public opinion is divided on its merits; and probably its designer, now that he discovers what his drawings really meant, may in this respect agree with the public." *The Quarterly Review*, April, 1872.
Drawn by A. S. Cook.

The Albert Hall, a huge circular structure of brick, with a shallow dome, impressively simple in form, and discreetly decorated externally in terra-cotta and mosaic. Built between 1867 and 1871, to the design of Captain Fowke (1823–65), and carried out after Fowke's death by Major-General Scott (1822–83). *Drawn by David Owen.*

spirit and power—as they dance and sing—with a certain mingling of vanity . . . like the feeling in which a child builds a tower of cards; and, in nobler instances, with also a strong sense of, and delight in, the majesty, height, and strength of the building itself, such as we have in a lofty tree or a peaked mountain."

Innumerable little brothers of Colcutt's thrusting array of towers and pinnacles and domes, sprouted and budded as additions to old houses or as features of new buildings, all over Britain. There were also rather blunted but comfortable-looking versions of classic architecture, corpulent in detail and solid in effect, like the façade of the Garrick Club in Garrick Street, and the adjoining buildings. Designed by Frederick Marrable, superintending architect to the Metropolitan Board of Works, the Club's premises were opened in 1864. (See plate 8.) A few buildings achieved originality, and of these the Albert Hall with its impressively simple form and discreet external decoration, was one of the most outstanding. Built between 1867 and 1871, it was designed by Captain Francis Fowke (1823–65), and carried out after his death by Major-General Henry Young Darracott Scott

The court of the Victoria and Albert Museum, South Kensington, designed by Captain Francis Fowke (1823–65). It was begun the year after Fowke's death, and completed, like the Albert Hall, by Major-General Henry Young Darracott Scott (1822–83). The walls are of fine, deep red brick, and a large amount of pale cream terra-cotta, elaborately modelled, is used for external decoration. Pevsner suggests that the Early Renaissance Lombardic style was chosen by Fowke, probably under the influence of Gottfried Semper, a political refugee who had lived in London from 1849 to 1853, and enjoyed the favour of the Prince Consort. (The Buildings of England, *London: except the Cities of London and Westminster*, by Nikolaus Pevsner. Penguin Books, 1952, page 253.) The illustration above is reproduced, on a slightly reduced scale, from *Old and New London*, Volume V, by Edward Walford. (London: Cassell, Petter & Galpin, 1872–78.) Chapter IX, page 109. (See opposite, also page 105.)

(1822–83). This huge circular brick structure with its shallow dome of glass and iron has a Roman stateliness; the bold composition reasserts the vitality of the classic tradition, and it is significant that it was conceived and completed by two engineers. (See pages 105 and above.)

The true architects of the Victorian period were the engineers, who were also the first industrial designers, unconscious of their own originality, inclined to be apologetic about the practical character of the bridges and tunnels, railway stations and factories they built, even feeling obliged to apply Gothic

The Huxley Building, Exhibition Road, South Kensington, designed by Captain Fowke, and begun and completed after his death by Major-General Scott, 1868–73 (See opposite and page 105.) Reproduced from plate 43, *Old and New London*, Volume V, by Edward Walford. (London: Cassell, Petter & Galpin, 1872–78.)

or classic trimmings to the authentic contemporary style they were creating. For example, Sir Robert Rawlinson (1810–98), a distinguished civil engineer, published a book of *Designs for Factory, Furnace, and other Tall Chimneys* in 1862, which gave directions for disguising such structures in various styles.[117] Two of his designs, shown on page 109, are inferior in character to the unpretentious standpipe and chimney on page 108, built in 1857 for the Grand Junction Water Works Company on Campden Hill, Kensington, by

The standpipe and chimney tower on Campden Hill, Kensington, built for the Grand Junction Water Works Company in 1857. Designed by Alexander Fraser, M.I.C.E. (1823–95), who later became engineer to the Company, it was constructed by John Aird (1800–76), one of the great Victorian public works contractors, whose son, Sir John Aird, Bart. (1833–1911), was associated with him and carried on the business after his death. Its unpretentious Italianate character has far more distinction than the examples in Sir Robert Rawlinson's book, which was published in 1862. (See opposite page.) *Drawn by Hilton Wright.*

Two examples from Sir Robert Rawlinson's *Designs for Factory, Furnace, and other Tall Chimneys*, published in 1862, and apparently printed privately for the author. Reviewing this work, *The Art Journal* (1862, pages 57–59) said of the designs reproduced here that the one on the right "is a ventilating (or a chimney) shaft, adapted for a baronial residence, or for some of those magnificent mercantile establishments that are now frequently built in the baronial style." The other "recalls reminiscences of the well-known campanile at Verona."

Left: Congleton Viaduct, on the North Staffordshire line, which carried the track 114 feet above the bed of the river on ten brick arches with a span of 50 feet. Designed by J. C. Forsyth and opened in 1849.

Below: The bridge at Maidenhead, designed by I. K. Brunel, to take the Great Western line over the Thames. The two main elliptical arches have a span of 130 feet. Reproduced from *Our Iron Roads*, by Frederick S. Williams. London: 1852.

Alexander Fraser, M.I.C.E. (1823–95), an Italianate tower, immortalised by G. K. Chesterton in *The Napoleon of Notting Hill*.

Early railway architecture had direct continuity with the classic system of design, and it was natural and perhaps obvious for Brunel to build the portals of the Box Tunnel on the Great Western Railway like Roman triumphal arches, towering above the broad gauge line, symbolic of the triumphant new power of steam. Few men of genius have had the opportunity of creating the environment for a completely new social and mechanical change; and such an opportunity came to Isambard Kingdom Brunel (1806–59), when, at the age of twenty-seven, he was appointed engineer to the newly projected Great Western Railway. Like the architects of the Georgian Age, he was a master designer; he assumed responsibility for the form and character of everything connected with the railway—stations, signals, bridges and tunnels: he gave coherence to the railway landscape, and like all great designers had an impeccable sense of style. This relieved him of dependence upon any particular architectural fashion; he chose what seemed appropriate to accord with his design: he did not adjust his design to the needs of any accepted style; and he reunited in his work the long-separated functions of architect and engineer.

Although there were few precedents for railway architecture, the entrances to tunnels suggested classical or mediaeval prototypes—not because, like Brunel, a designer wanted an arched portal in the grand classical manner, but for more grave and solid reasons. In *Our Iron Roads*, first issued in 1852, Frederick S. Williams said that such portals "should be massive, to be suitable as approaches to works presenting the appearance of gloom, solidity, and strength."[118] He said that plainness when combined with boldness, and massiveness without heaviness, constituted elegance in a tunnel entrance: it was also most economical. "These conditions," he added, "may be answered without cramping the taste of the engineer, as far as taste enters into the composition of such designs; for architectural display in such works would be as misplaced as the massiveness of engineering works would be, if applied

COMPONENTS OF
THE RAILWAY
LANDSCAPE

Left: Station signal, with cottage.
Right: Junction signals.
Below: Level-crossing. In America it was called a grade-crossing.

Reproduced on a reduced scale from *Our Iron Roads*, by Frederick S. Williams. London: 1852.

Cuttings and embankments altered the character of the countryside, but seldom disfigured the face of the land: they stretched ribbons of grass and wild flowers beside the tracks. Reproduced from *Our Iron Roads*, by Frederick S. Williams. London: 1852.

to the elegant and tastefully-designed structures of the architect." Such confused thinking suggests why engineers were inclined to be diffident about the aesthetic merits of their work, and how impossible it was for them to identify their structures as the authentic architecture of their age. Williams illustrated the mouth of the Shugborough Park tunnel in *Our Iron Roads* (reproduced opposite), and the portals, in common with other bridge structures in the vicinity, were designed to meet the requirements of the Earl of Lichfield, who as a great local landholder could impose such conditions. "The north face of this structure," said Williams, "forms a noble archway, deeply moulded, flanked by two square towers, the whole being surmounted by a battlemented parapet. The lofty trees, covered with the richest foliage, rising from the elevated ground through which the tunnel is pierced, give a depth of tone and artistic effect to the whole scene at once imposing and beautiful, and form a remarkably fine feature in the scenery of the railway."[119] The northern mouth of Ipswich Tunnel on what was formerly the Eastern Union Railway is of comparable design, and was, as Mr. Hamilton Ellis has suggested, "designed to give nervous passengers a reassuring impression of great

Tunnel entrances were intimidating, and were designed intentionally to "be suitable as approaches to works presenting the appearance of gloom, solidity, and strength." This view was expressed by Frederick S. Williams in *Our Iron Roads*, first published in 1852. Referring to the illustration reproduced above from that work, he wrote: "The appearance of the mouths of some tunnels, especially when thrown out into prominent relief by a pleasant and well-wooded landscape stretching around and behind them, is by no means unattractive. As proof of this statement, a better illustration could scarcely be furnished than that of the Shugborough Park tunnel, on the Trent Valley Railway. The north face of this structure forms a noble archway, deeply moulded, flanked by two square towers, the whole being surmounted by a battlemented parapet. The lofty trees, covered with the richest foliage, rising from the elevated ground through which the tunnel is pierced, give a depth of tone and artistic effect to the whole scene at once imposing and beautiful, and form a remarkably fine feature in the scenery of the railway." The portals of this tunnel, in common with other bridge structures in the vicinity, were designed to meet the requirements of the Earl of Lichfield. The south face is a severely classical arch, with rusticated voussoirs.

Above: Eastern Counties Railway Station, Cambridge, by Sancton Wood, 1844–45. This is a piece of unpretentious Victorian classic, using traditional building techniques. From *The Illustrated London News*, August 2nd, 1845. *Below:* The sheds at Paddington Station, designed jointly by I. K. Brunel and Matthew Digby Wyatt, 1852–54. A new architecture of cast and wrought iron and glass is emerging. From *The Illustrated London News*, July 8th, 1854.

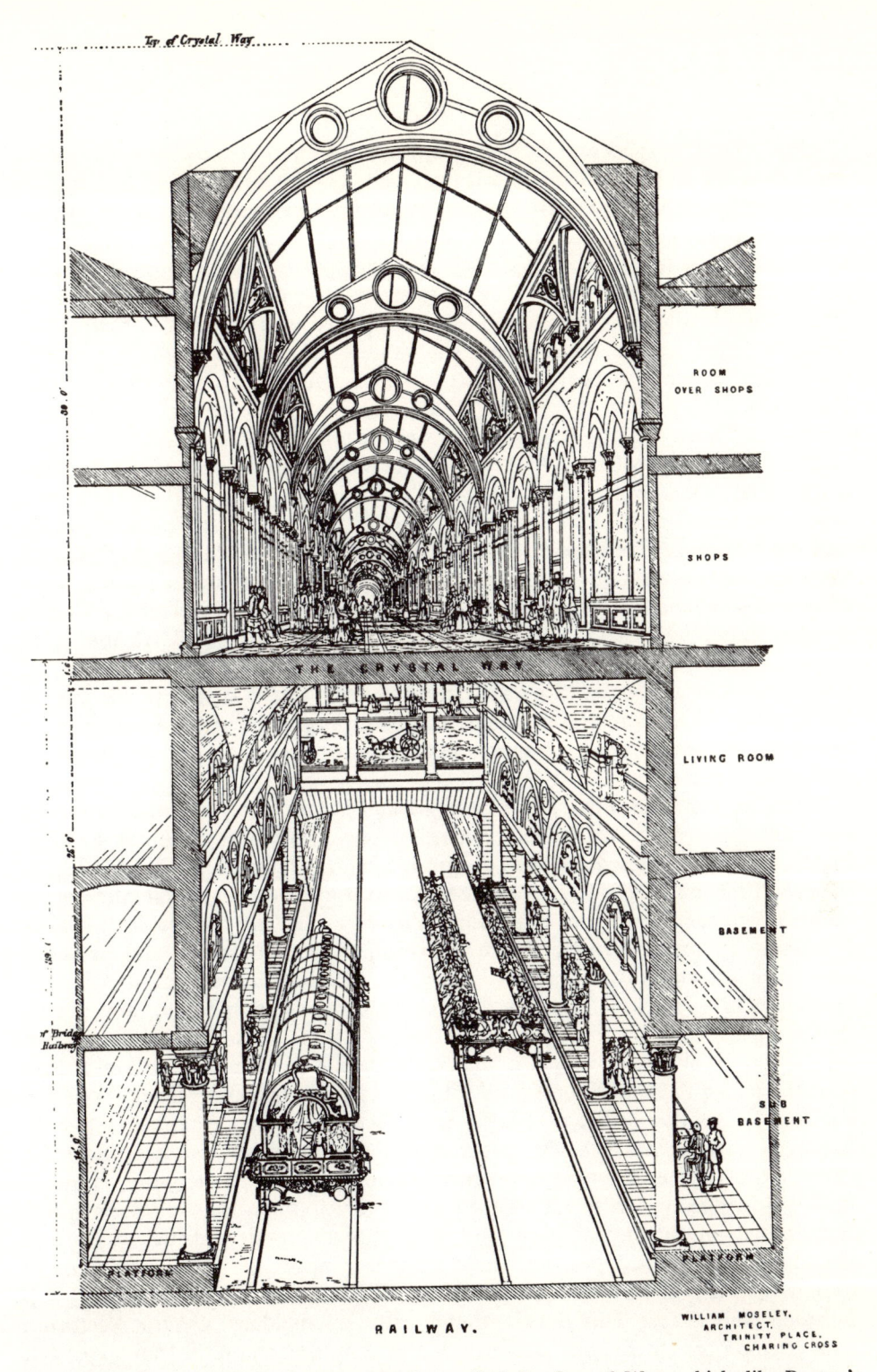

A glass arcade, designed by William Moseley, called the Crystal Way, which, like Paxton's idea for a great Victorian Way, was to encircle London, with a railway at the lowest level, passing under streets, and a high level shopping arcade for pedestrians only, with a glass roof. (See page 134.) From the printed report ordered by the House of Commons, July 23rd, 1855.
Reproduced by courtesy of the Trustees of the British Museum.

solidity."[120] The road and railway bridges of the period show how the latent contemporary style was usually frustrated by loyalty to traditional materials and shapes or a dramatic attachment to antique or mediaeval styles. When Brunel won the competition for the bridge at Clifton in 1829, his project was to cross the 200 foot deep gorge with a single span, 700 feet long, suspended by chains which were supported by piers formed like gigantic Egyptian pylons. The Clifton bridge was not completed and opened until 1863, four years after Brunel's death, and it incorporated the chains and ironwork from another of his bridges which was opened in 1845 and crossed the Thames from behind Hungerford Market to the Surrey side. (See plates 16 and 17.) Originally known as Charing Cross Bridge, this was the first suspension bridge erected in the Metropolitan area. The Italianate suspension towers rose from two brick piers, which were retained when the bridge was removed in 1860, and now bear the girders of the railway bridge. The first Charing Cross bridge and the Clifton bridge were not inert copies of Italianate and Egyptian forms; the suspension towers on both were built of traditional materials, which were successfully married to wrought-iron, as they were in William Tierney Clark's suspension bridge at Hammersmith, which was built between 1824 and 1827 with two heavy masonry towers that looked like plinths for colossal statues. Clark's bridge was replaced in 1887 by one built to the design of Sir Joseph Bazalgette, with iron towers that were ill-proportioned and bloated in appearance, though actually much lighter than their masonry predecessors. (See page 121.)

Victorian combinations of cast- and wrought-iron with stone and brick did not fulfil the promise of the late Georgian bridge builders. Thomas Farnolls Pritchard, who designed the first cast-iron bridge, created a light and elegant structure, for architects then regarded cast-iron as a material that offered yet another convenient way of expressing the versatility of the classical idiom. His bridge spanned the Severn in Shropshire, between Madeley and Broseley, and was constructed by Abraham Darby, the Coalbrookdale ironfounder, who erected it in 1777–79. Although Pritchard's bridge had masonry abutments, they were an inconspicuous part of the design, for its character was determined by the nature of cast-iron as a structural material. (See opposite.) The bridge over the River Wear at Sunderland, built in 1796 to a modification of a design by Tom Paine, the author of *The Rights of Man*, is another example of a well-balanced partnership between cast-iron and traditional materials, and in the early years of the nineteenth century Thomas Telford and John Rastrick designed bridges which foreshadowed a new development of the classic tradition, based on the use of cast- and wrought-iron, and undistorted by any dependence on prototypes, for those engineers approached all problems of design with a typically Georgian sense of obligation to achieve stability with lightness and grace. This development was soon deflected by the Victorian insistence on ornament, and cast-iron was a tempting material that suggested

Above: The first cast-iron bridge in the world, designed by Thomas Farnolls Pritchard, an architect and builder of Shrewsbury, and erected in 1777–79. The material is used to create a light and elegant structure in the classical tradition of architectural design. From a drawing made from a steel engraving, *circa* 1782, in the possession of the Coalbrookdale Company.
Below: A cast-iron bridge over the River Aire at Leeds, designed by John and George Leather, civil engineers, and opened in July, 1841. This lacks the simplicity and elegance of the early cast-iron bridges. From *The Official Catalogue of the Great Exhibition*, 1851, Volume I, page 323.

Chelsea Bridge, designed by Thomas Page, was opened to the public in March, 1858. The four towers were 97 feet high. Originally gilded and painted to represent light-coloured bronze, they were surmounted by large globular lamps. Reproduced from *The Illustrated London News*, April 10th, 1858.

decorative extravagances, curbed in complexity only by the limitations of the casting process.

For example, the bridge over the River Aire at Leeds, shown on page 117, designed by John and George Leather and opened in 1841, is maladroit by comparison with the early cast-iron bridges, and lacks the simplicity of form and airy elegance of Telford's work, or of Rastrick's bridge over the Wye at Chepstow. Some of the Victorian suspension bridges achieved a spurious elegance, and of these Albert Bridge, which spans the Thames from Chelsea to Battersea, is mildly loyal to the Gothic taste, for the cast-iron towers suggest the restraint of eighteenth-century fashion rather than the fervours of the Revival. It was obviously a metal bridge, and, unlike Chelsea and Hammersmith bridges, was not oppressed by decorative features. (See pages 120 and 121.)

Continuation of view of the original Chelsea suspension bridge. This gay and decorative structure was replaced in 1934 by the present conventionally functional design. Bazalgette's suspension bridge at Hammersmith, opened twenty-nine years later, lacks the boldness and classical character of Page's design. (See page 121.)

Bridges that carried railways over rivers and across valleys invited frankness in design, but although men like Brunel accepted the invitation, and produced such outstanding works as the Royal Albert Bridge at Saltash, others were content with a compromise between iron and masonry in some traditional style. The Saltash Bridge, opened in 1859, is a perfect example of the style that engineers were creating, and critics and architects were either ignoring or denigrating. (See plate 17.) Ten years earlier, Robert Stephenson had built the Britannia Bridge over the Menai Strait, consisting of two independent continuous tubular beams, supported at five places, on the abutments and on three towers. In a detailed description of the construction Samuel Smiles said: "The design of the masonry is such as to accord with the form of the tubes, being somewhat of an Egyptian character, massive and gigantic rather than beautiful, but bearing the unmistakable impress of power."[121] Although it

Albert Bridge, which spans the Thames from Chelsea to Battersea, was designed by Rowland Mason Ordish (1824–86), a civil engineer who was obviously influenced by the Gothic taste, though the cast-iron towers that bear the marks of it suggest the modish restraint of eighteenth-century fashion rather than the fervours of the Revival. It was opened in September, 1873, and cost about £200,000 to build: eleven years later its condition caused anxiety, and the suspension members of the structure were overhauled and various alterations made under the direction of Sir Joseph William Bazalgette (1819–91), chief engineer of the Metropolitan Board of Works. The historical and descriptive notes on *Bridges*, published by the London County Council, states that "the whole structure is, from an engineering point of view, very unsatisfactory, although the height and lightness of construction of the towers, which are 101 feet high (above high water), give the bridge an attractive appearance." (Second edition, 1914, page 10.) The bridge has a spurious elegance, but when its demolition was first suggested in 1956, a sentimental uproar followed, and it was defended with the passion that is reserved in Britain for indifferent architecture or inconvenient structures. Sir Joseph Bazalgette, who was called in to ensure that the bridge continued to stand up, would have been astonished at the fuss. *Drawn by David Owen.*

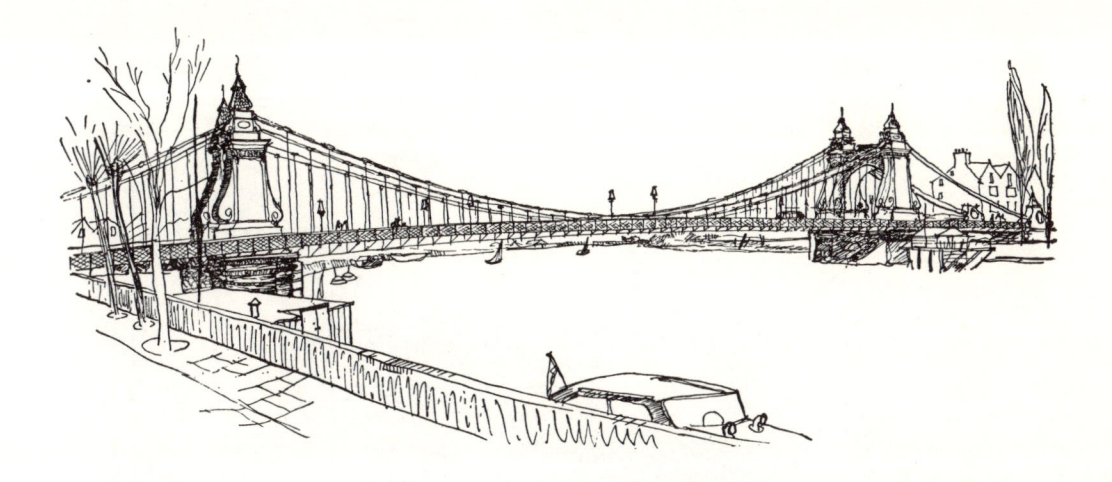

Above: Hammersmith Bridge, designed by Sir Joseph Bazalgette, and opened on June 18th, 1887. *Drawn by Hilton Wright*. This structure, with its light, wrought-iron towers and steel chains, replaced the suspension bridge shown below, which was designed by William Tierney Clark (1782–1852), and erected 1824–27. It was the first suspension bridge to cross the Thames near London.

The railway bridge that crosses the Mersey from Runcorn to Widnes. The lattice girders are carried on stone piers, high above the river level, and allowing clearance for ships passing along the Manchester Ship Canal, which at this point follows the Cheshire bank of the Mersey. The masonry is designed with a mediaeval fortress in mind: and the so-called "castellated style" was presumed to confer "the appearance of gloom, solidity, and strength" which was considered correct for the entrances to tunnels. (See page 111.) This bridge, completed in May, 1868, was designed by William Baker, Chief Engineer of the London and North Western Railway, and Francis Stevenson, Assistant Engineer. *Drawn by David Owen.*

was considered a marvel of the age, "one of the most wonderful structures of modern times," according to the author of *Our Iron Roads*, it was essentially a compromise. The pseudo-Egyptian towers were not bold, impressive pylons like those on Brunel's Clifton bridge, but deliberately intended to impart an air of solid strength, which comforted railway passengers by increasing their sense of security. Anything that looked as heavy as the Britannia Bridge *must* be safe. (See opposite page.) The railway bridge that crosses the Mersey from Runcorn to Widnes is another compromise between traditional and industrial materials, intentionally ponderous, with masonry in the so-called "castellated style," and as intimidating as a mediaeval fortress. Designed by William Baker, chief engineer of the London and North Western Railway, and Francis Stevenson, assistant engineer, it was opened in 1868. (See opposite page.)

Sir Benjamin Baker and Sir John Fowler, the designers of the Forth Bridge, used 38,000 tons of steel to create a new form of bridge architecture. Here was the characteristic style of the industrial age, a frank acknowledgment of steel construction, as Brunel's Saltash bridge had been a frank acknowledgment of wrought-iron construction—uninhibited and endowed with a new elegance. But it was engineering, which most people believed to be something separate and apart from architecture. This was naked metal, exposing a skeleton to the world; there was nothing solid and lush about steel, nothing that could be forced into fluid forms, like cast-iron. There was something almost indecent about such purposeful framework, and in structures like the Tower Bridge the steelwork was concealed. (See pages 124 and 125.)

A false and complex style developed from the use of cast-iron. It was false, because its basic purpose was to be ornamental at all costs; it was complex because of the reckless borrowing of Renaissance, Gothic and Byzantine ornaments, which were intermingled without any sense of restraint or proportion

The Britannia Bridge over the Menai Strait, designed by Robert Stephenson and completed in 1849. Like the Runcorn Bridge on the opposite page, this was a compromise between the new industrial materials and traditional masonry. Railway engineers felt obliged to impart an air of strength to their structures by the use of ancient architectural forms: mediaeval on the Runcorn Bridge, pseudo-Egyptian on this example. *Drawn from an engraving formerly in the possession of the London, Midland and Scottish Railway.*

VICTORIAN TASTE

Design for a chain bridge to cross the Firth of Forth, described in a pamphlet by James Anderson, a civil engineer and surveyor, which was published in Edinburgh in 1818. It was the first of many designs for a Forth bridge. The profile of the bridge that was begun in 1882 and completed in 1889 is shown below. Reproduced from an article on "The Forth Bridge," by W. Westhofen, published in *Engineering*, February 28th, 1890.

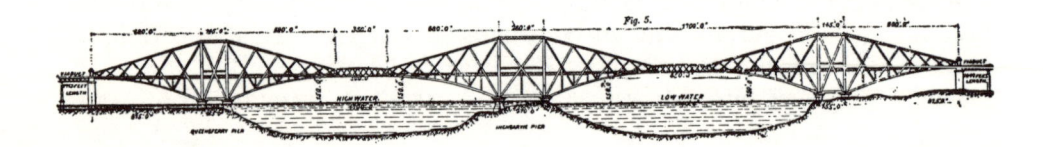

General view of the Forth Bridge, designed by Sir Benjamin Baker (1840–1907) and Sir John Fowler (1817–98). *Drawn by Hilton Wright, A.R.I.B.A.*, and reproduced from *Guide to Western Architecture*, by courtesy of George Allen & Unwin Ltd.

The miasmic influence of the Gothic Revival persisted to the end of the period, and as late as 1895 such structures as the Tower Bridge exhibited incongruous mixtures of contemporary engineering and mediaeval features. The main towers and the abutment towers have steel skeletons hidden by stone facing, backed with brickwork. Such absurd forms of disguise were applauded, although the true style of the scientific industrial age had been proclaimed by such structures as the Crystal Palace and the Forth Bridge. *Drawn by Hilton Wright* and reproduced from *Guide to Western Architecture*, by courtesy of George Allen & Unwin Ltd.

with florid naturalistic motifs. Such a style satisfied the Victorian love of display, gratifying the eye by a parade of richness and technical skill, and becoming a visual ingredient of comfort. The value of cast-iron for ornamental work and the relaxation of the discipline usually imposed on metal workers that followed its extensive use, were described by Ewing Matheson, a civil engineer, writing in the 70's, who said that the material "may be made to any shape that plastic clay will take, or to any which can be carved in stone, marble, mahogany, or oak, it is nearly equal to hammered iron in giving delicacy of form. Moreover, some designs which are too delicate to be utilised in such materials as clay, stone and wood, are of sufficient strength if made in cast-iron. Herein lies its superiority over all other materials used in architecture; and this advantage is not lessened by the fact that another material —such as clay or wood—has to be temporarily employed in its production. Indeed, an art-workman has greater scope for design in the earlier stages of cast-iron manufacture (i.e. in the clay model) than in wrought-iron. It would, therefore, be unjust to deny to cast-iron the important place in the order of building materials which is now given to it by engineers and builders,

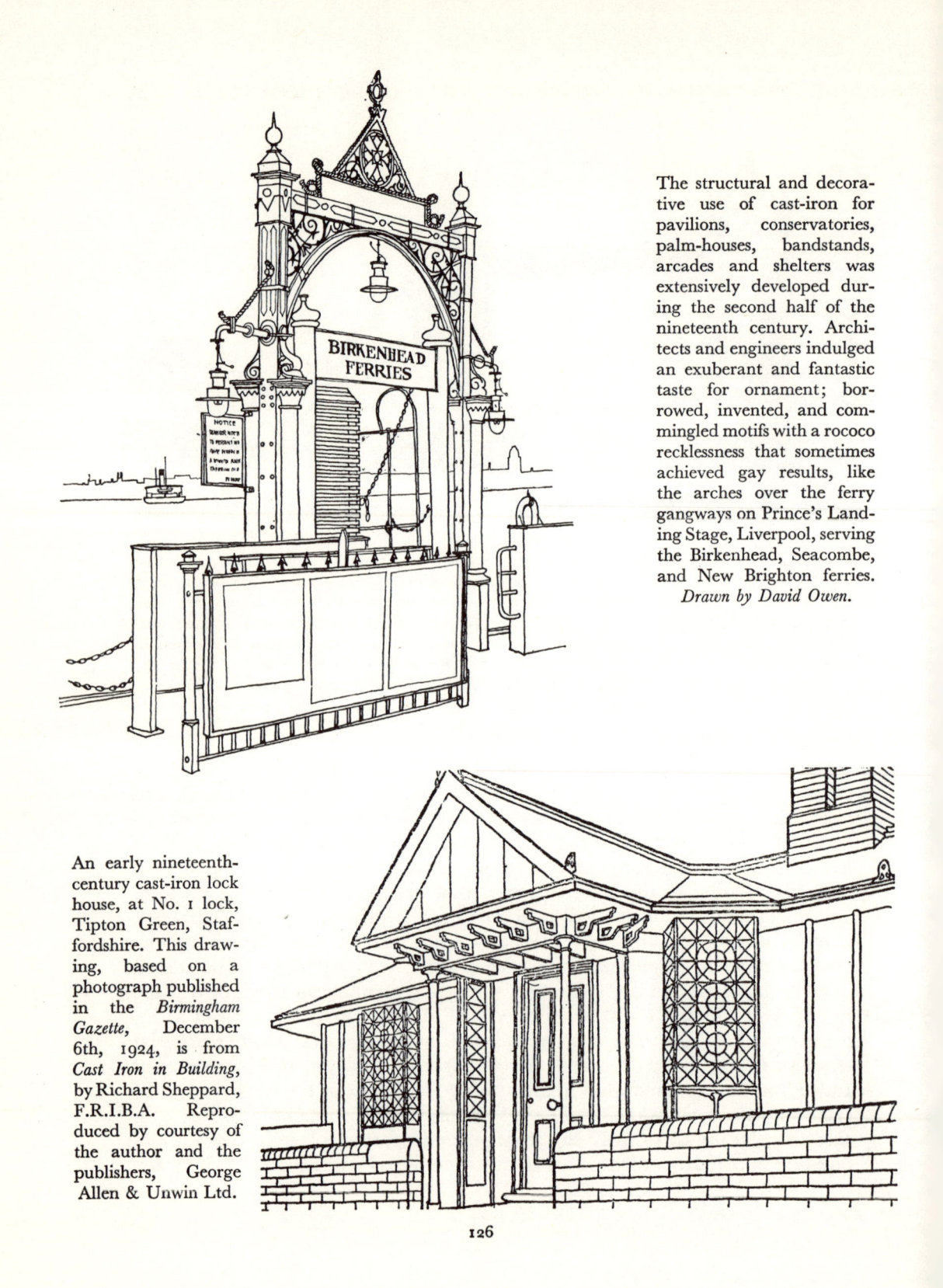

The structural and decorative use of cast-iron for pavilions, conservatories, palm-houses, bandstands, arcades and shelters was extensively developed during the second half of the nineteenth century. Architects and engineers indulged an exuberant and fantastic taste for ornament; borrowed, invented, and commingled motifs with a rococo recklessness that sometimes achieved gay results, like the arches over the ferry gangways on Prince's Landing Stage, Liverpool, serving the Birkenhead, Seacombe, and New Brighton ferries.
Drawn by David Owen.

An early nineteenth-century cast-iron lock house, at No. 1 lock, Tipton Green, Staffordshire. This drawing, based on a photograph published in the *Birmingham Gazette*, December 6th, 1924, is from *Cast Iron in Building*, by Richard Sheppard, F.R.I.B.A. Reproduced by courtesy of the author and the publishers, George Allen & Unwin Ltd.

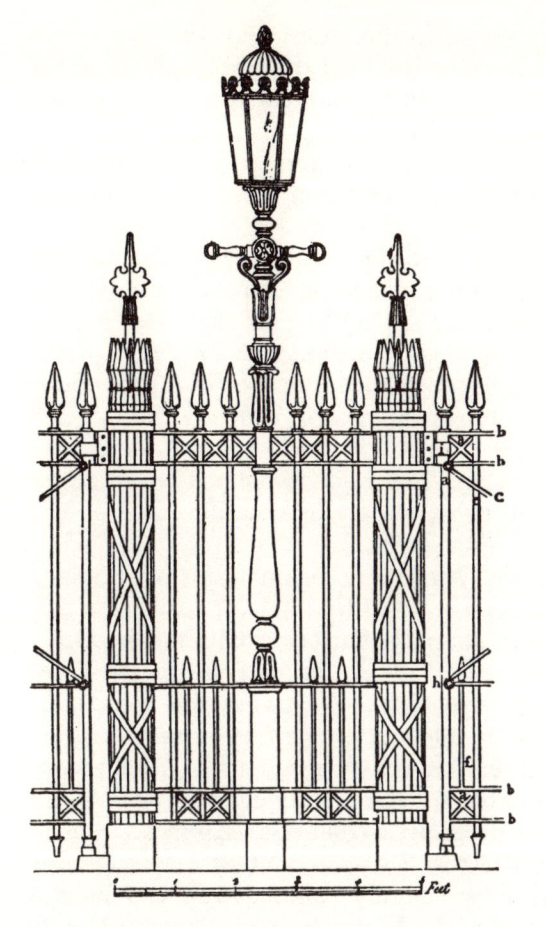

CAST-IRON STREET FURNITURE

The use of classic detail for lamp standards, gates, railings, fanlights, window guards for houses and shops, grilles below shop windows, balconies, newels and balusters for staircases was encouraged by the existence of a reliable and detailed copy-book, *The Smith and Founders' Director*, by L. N. Cottingham. Originally published in 1823, it went into several editions. Designs drawn from the plates of this book gave a Georgian dignity and purity of detail to much of the cast-iron work produced during the first half of the nineteenth century. *Left:* Details of a lamp and railings at Cumberland Gate, Hyde Park, London, reproduced from the 1840 edition.

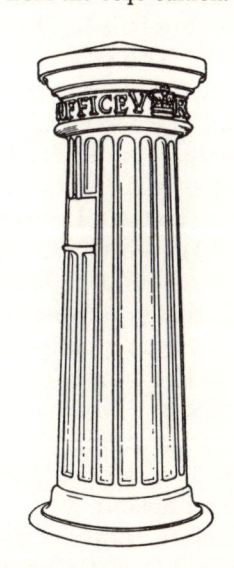

Right: The earliest letter-boxes were in the form of a Doric column, which explains why for a century the G.P.O. posting-boxes have been called "pillar-boxes." This example is from Banbury, Oxfordshire. *Drawn by Marcelle Barton from a photograph by the author.*

notwithstanding the aesthetical objections continually made to it by many architects. But although, as stated above, cast-iron can assume any form usual in wood, stone or clay, its peculiar qualities—hardness, sharpness, strength and durability—demand a new style of ornamentation. The attempts hitherto made at this, though constantly improving on the past, cannot be said to have perfected such a style; and as cast-iron is likely to maintain its position of utility, increasing success may be hoped for in the future. But while the merits of cast-iron are stated as above, it cannot be doubted that the quality and the rude appearance of many of the cheap castings supplied to builders in this country have justified considerable prejudice among architects, and have prevented the use of iron in many kinds of work where artistic ornament is desired, and where, if properly manufactured, cast-iron should be adopted to great advantage."[122]

The "aesthetical objections" of architects to the material were strengthened by many of the exhibits at the Great Exhibition of 1851, such as the ornamental dome shown opposite, which was condemned as "one of the most pretentious works in the Building" by an anonymous contributor to *The Crystal Palace and its Contents*, who said: "The casting supports the reputation of the founders; but there are many and grave objections to the design, which is childish and purposeless. Though called a dome, it is merely a rustic garden house. . . . Within is a cast of J. Bell's 'Eagle Slayer.' The eagle transfixed by an arrow at the top inside must be considered an absolutely inexcusable piece of bad taste."[123]

The use of cast-iron by architects like Nash and Rickman, for reproducing classic columns or Gothic tracery, though scorned by Pugin and other purists, was very different from the decorative anarchy that occurred after the Great Exhibition. The structural and ornamental use of the material for pavilions, bandstands and the columns and superstructure of piers at seaside resorts, for palm-houses, conservatories and arcades, allowed a taste for coarse decoration to be cheaply indulged. Motifs from every known style were used with a rococo recklessness, sometimes with gay results, like the ferry gangways on Prince's Landing Stage at Liverpool, where decorative confusion is imposed on an orderly framework. (See page 126.) Richard Sheppard in *Cast Iron in Building* has observed that "Most of our piers are highly characteristic and have a genius of design all their own; they were the Victorian equivalent of the folk festival, and the quality of their decoration is expressive; it is bold, coarse and vigorous. The iron is used flamboyantly in panels and columns and crockets and gables, for windows and doors, for turnstiles and slot machines. Buried under the paint and obscured by later accretions the social investigator can discover a record of the habits, characteristics and amusements of mid-Victorian England."[124]

The classic tradition emerged sporadically: the earliest letter-boxes were dwarf fluted Doric columns of cast-iron (see page 127), and the girders of road and railway bridges were often borne by cast-iron columns, generally of the Tuscan order, which were also used in an elongated form in the interior of Euston Station, and, with more robust proportions, at Lime Street, Liverpool (see plate 15). In Paddington Station, designed jointly by Brunel and Matthew Digby Wyatt, cast-iron columns supported the roof, but the ornamental treatment was contributed by Wyatt. (See page 114.) Brunel had conceived

Ornamental iron dome, cast by the Coalbrookdale Company, and shown at the Great Exhibition, 1851. From *The Crystal Palace and its Contents*, page 89.

the terminus building as "entirely *metal* as to all the general forms, arrangements and design" and said, in his letter to Wyatt inviting collaboration, that "it almost of necessity becomes an Engineering Work, but, to be honest, even if it were not, it is a branch of architecture of which I am fond, and, *of course*, believe myself fully competent for; but for *detail* of ornamentation I neither have time nor knowledge, and with all my confidence in my own ability I have never any objection to advice and assistance even in the department which I keep to myself, namely the general design. Now, in this building which, *entre nous*, will be one of the largest of its class, I want to carry out,

General view of the exterior of the Great Exhibition building in Hyde Park. From *Old and New London*, Volume V, by Edward Walford. (London: Cassell, Petter & Galpin, 1872–78.) Chapter II, page 31. (See opposite page.)

strictly and fully, all those correct notions of the use of metal which I believe you and I share (except that I should carry them still farther than you) and I think will be a nice opportunity."(125)

The ornamental details of the columns, while admirably suited to the casting process, suggest an oriental model, but the general effect of the interior fulfils Brunel's desire that it should be entirely metal, and that the design should express the properties of the material. Such buildings of iron and glass were tentative expressions of the true, unrecognised style of the period, although Ruskin had assumed in *The Seven Lamps of Architecture*, that "true architecture does not admit iron as a constructive material, and that such works as the cast-iron central spire of Rouen Cathedral, or the iron roofs and pillars of our railway stations, and of some of our churches, are not architecture at all."

Above: The south façade of the Crystal Palace, showing the principal entrance to the Exhibition.
Below: Interior view from the South Entrance. Reproduced from *The Official Catalogue*, Volume I, page 51 and plate 25.

With one of those flashes of prophetic insight which so often contradicted his dogmatic assertions and prejudices, Ruskin had also said, "the time is probably near when a new system of architectural laws will be developed, adapted entirely to metallic construction." But he qualified the statement by adding: "I believe that the tendency of all present sympathy and association is to limit the idea of architecture to non-metallic work...."

The greatest of all buildings of iron and glass was the Crystal Palace, which gave expression to the Industrial Revolution in terms of architectural design and also began the structural revolution from which a new form of Western architecture would arise. Designed by Joseph Paxton to house the Great Exhibition of 1851, it was constructed of prefabricated units of cast- and wrought-iron and glass, and when it was erected in Hyde Park it was admired as a wonder of the age, or contemptuously referred to as an outsize greenhouse. Very naturally it infuriated Ruskin who proclaimed that iron and glass were "eternally separated from all good and great things by a gulf which not all the tubular bridges nor engineering of ten thousand nineteenth centuries cast into one great bronze-foreheaded century will ever overpass one inch of." But nobody, not even its designer, was aware that a new form of architecture had been created—the progenitor of building techniques which were to influence not only British but European and American architecture for a century. Joseph

Sir Charles Fox (1810–74), engineer, whose firm, Fox, Henderson & Co., undertook the contract for the Crystal Palace. Fox was a gifted engineer, and had introduced the use of the switch on railway tracks in place of the sliding rail. He was knighted for his work on the Crystal Palace. The severity of his expression in this portrait, reproduced from *The Crystal Palace and its Contents* (page 32), suggests that it was drawn before his resentment at Paxton's knighthood was soothed by receiving his own. (See opposite page.)

Sir Joseph Paxton (1801–65), the designer of the Crystal Palace which housed the Great Exhibition of 1851. (Reproduced from *The Crystal Palace and its Contents*, London: 1852.) There is reason to believe that there were differences of opinion about who should take the credit for the design. The Rev. Fitzwilliam Taylor, who was present at the opening of the Exhibition on May 1st, 1851, included the following observations in his account of the proceedings: "As the Queen moved to the middle of the building, a spray of water flowed from a fountain in the roof. Two gentlemen in front of us were gesticulating and shouting at each other in an angry way. I found out that one was Sir Joseph Paxton, who designed the plan last year, and was knighted by the Queen: the other was a Mr. Fox, who actually designed the building, and I suppose he thought he should be knighted also. (I think he was in the end.)" This account is quoted in *Combat and Carnival*, by Peter Carew. (London: Constable & Co., 1954, page 123.) Mr. Fox's firm, Fox, Henderson & Co., were the contractors, whose tender of £79,800 was accepted by the Commissioners. (*Official Catalogue*, Volume I, Introduction, page 21.) (See page opposite.)

Paxton (1801–65) had, like Loudon, been a gardener who became interested in architecture. He was employed by the Duke of Devonshire as superintendent of the gardens and grounds of Chatsworth and manager of the Duke's Derbyshire estates. He originated the idea of the Great Conservatory at Chatsworth, which was probably designed by Decimus Burton, and built 1836–40 (plate 18), and the Palm House at Kew, designed by Decimus Burton and Richard Turner, begun in 1844, was another development of the curvilinear glazing technique invented by Loudon.

Although the Crystal Palace was one of the ancestors of the new Western architecture, Paxton, a true Victorian, was blissfully unconscious of his real achievement; he had no idea that he had fathered an entirely fresh form of architecture, and when his fame and success brought him commissions for

The Metropolitan Meat Market at Smithfield, designed by Sir Horace Jones (1819–87), the City architect, begun in 1867 and opened in November, 1868. Reproduced from an engraving in *Old and New London*, Volume II, edited by Walter Thornbury, who described it as "a huge parallelogram, 631 feet long and 246 feet wide" which covered $3\frac{1}{2}$ acres. "It was not over-beautiful," he observed, "but then its necessities were peculiar and imperative. The style would probably be called Italian, but it resembles more the Renaissance of France, that style which mediaevalists shudder at, but which is more elastic in the architect's hands than the Gothic." He did not observe that in this huge building of iron and glass, the unrecognised style of the age was struggling to be free. (Pages 493–94.) (London: Cassell, Petter & Galpin, 1872–78.)

other works he executed them in a flabby version of the classical style. When his imagination was stimulated, he produced original ideas of which one was a project for a vast iron and glass arcade, eleven and a half miles long, that was to encircle London. It was to be called the Great Victorian Way and was intended to improve metropolitan communications. The proposal, and many others like it, was examined by a committee set up by the House of Commons, but did not outlive the preliminary discussions. (See page 115.)

The adventurous experiments with contemporary materials and new techniques of construction were seldom noted by architects who were far too busy fighting in the Battle of the Styles. So the authentic architecture of the period was rarely identified, though it altered the character of cities and changed the face of the land. Tennyson was moved to celebrate the momentous triumphs of engineering in the opening verses of *Mechanophilus*:

> "Now first we stand and understand,
> And sunder false from true,
> And handle boldly with the hand,
> And see and shape and do.
>
> "Dash back that ocean with a pier,
> Strow yonder mountain flat,
> A railway there, a tunnel here,
> Mix me this Zone with that!"

While Brunel and Robert Stephenson might have touched their hats in perfunctory acknowledgment of such sentiments, most architects, and indeed most people, were incapable of sundering "false from true." But enterprising engineers and industrialists by mixing "this Zone with that," created the unsure image of a new world.

This decoration, depicting George Stephenson, and the device used as a chapter heading on page 101, are reproduced from *The Rocket, or The Story of the Stephensons, Father and Son*, by H. C. Knight. (London: Thomas Nelson & Sons, 1880.)

CHAPTER VII

ORNAMENT AND DESIGN

WHEN the architectural background of social and civic life ceased to be orderly, and became convulsive and chaotic as a result of conflicting loyalties to various styles, the use of ornament was unregulated by any disciplined sense of restraint. Ruskin had given his approbation to the free use of natural ornament; the Gothic revival encouraged the proliferation of naturalistic motifs; and the formalised acanthus leaves, honeysuckle, and geometric patterns that enriched the components of the classic orders were either discarded or distorted. Ornament and design became confused, and after the Great Exhibition of 1851 the Victorian love of ornament for its own sake was immoderately indulged. Ornament appeased the anxious appetite of the new rich and the prosperous middle classes for visible evidence of their social status, and gave many people not only innocent pleasure, but draped a curtain of fantasy over the realities of life, as conventional respectability draped a curtain, less fantastic but far thicker, over the crude facts and aberrant lusts of human nature.

The purposeless pursuit of ornamental effects, and the consequent degradation of the form and function of nearly everything people used, disturbed a few clear-sighted writers and critics, and of these Ralph Nicholson Wornum (1812–77) was one of the most lucid. He was Keeper and Secretary of the National Gallery, a portrait painter, a lecturer and an art critic. In his best known work, *Analysis of Ornament*, first published in 1856, he described and illustrated some of the results that occasionally followed the enthusiastic use of naturalistic motifs. Three of the examples he gave are reproduced on page 138, and they show how designers had, by subordinating form and function wholly to the interests of ornament, parted with their common sense. "The great art of the designer," he wrote, "is in the selection and arrangement of his materials, not in their execution. There is a distinct *study of ornament* wholly independent of the merely preliminary exercises of drawing, colouring, or modelling. A designer might even produce a perfect arrangement of forms and colours, and yet show the grossest stupidity in its application."[126] Stupidity of this kind, all too common, was encouraged by the absence of valid critical standards, though ornament copied directly from nature was at least a refreshing change from the intricacies of that debased style of interior decoration and furnishing which, originating in Germany after the Napoleonic wars, was called Biedermier. The name was taken from a Philistine character popularised in the journal *Fliegende Blätter*. It was really a vulgarised version of the French Empire style, depending on the lavish use of carved wood and composition and embossed metal, and when it reached England it overcrowded every surface with its luscious complexities. But there was no governing framework, no system of design, to keep ornamental fashions in order, as all kinds of exotic fashions, Rococo, Chinese, and Indian, had been kept in order during the Georgian period by the universal adoption of the classic idiom.

Writing of the rise of the *naturalist* school of ornament, Wornum said: "The theory appears to be, that as nature is beautiful, ornamental details derived immediately from beautiful natural objects must insure a beautiful design. This, however, can only be true where the original uses of the details chosen have not been obviously violated; and one peculiar feature of this school is, that it often substitutes the *ornament* itself for the thing to be ornamented, as illustrated in the accompanying examples [see page 138]; in which the natural objects are so mismanaged as to be *principals*: flame proceeding from a flower, a basket on an animal's head to hold a liquid, a bell made of leaves! the elements chosen being so opposed to the proposed uses of the objects ornamented, as to make the designs simply aesthetic monstrosities, ornamental abominations."[127]

The excessive ornamentation of nearly every article used in the Victorian home made even the spacious rooms of large houses seem overcrowded, and in small rooms the effect was overwhelming: yet this excess of ornament, this restless conflict of motifs, helped to create an atmosphere of solid, unshakable comfort. Harriet Beecher Stowe, who visited England in 1853, said of English hosts that "the matter of coziness and home comfort has been so studied, and matured, and reduced to system, that they really have it in their power to effect more, towards making their guests comfortable, than perhaps any other people."[128] In the reception room that had been prepared for her at "a beautiful little retreat, on the banks of the Mersey, called the 'Dingle,' " she was delighted to find that "no item of cozy comfort that one could desire was omitted." The words *cozy* and *comfort* were always being used together: they could never have been applied to the well-proportioned, elegantly furnished interiors of the Georgian period (the word cozy was not in general use in the eighteenth century), though they seemed appropriate for the Elizabethan style which the Victorians revived with sumptuous additions and variations. Without intemperance in decoration, coziness and comfort might have deserted the Victorian interior. Perhaps a few people would have agreed with Wornum that: "Ornament is essentially the accessory to, and not the substitute of, the useful; it is a decoration or adornment; it can have no independent existence practically."[129] But popular admiration was lavished on the exhibits at the Crystal Palace, and many of these completely contradicted Wornum's view

138   VICTORIAN TASTE

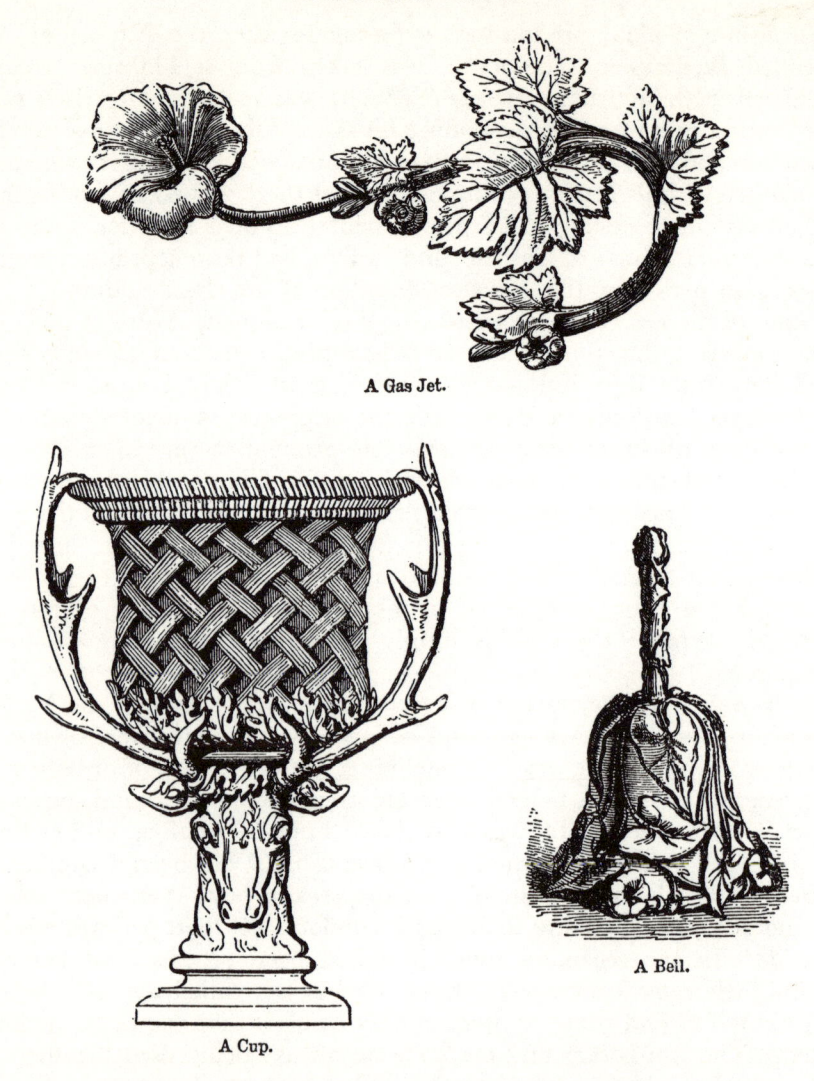

A Gas Jet.

A Cup.

A Bell.

Three examples given by Wornum in his *Analysis of Ornament* to show how "natural objects are so mismanaged as to be *principals*. . . ."

that "every implement or article of practical utility, as, for instance, a candlestick, that is composed or built up of natural imitations exclusively or as principals, however practical the idea may be supposed to be is practically bad in design."[130] The stork candelabrum, in bronze, by William Potts of Birmingham, on the opposite page, shows how involved this building up process could become.

Right: The stork candelabrum, by William Potts of Birmingham. The brass and bronze work shown by Potts at the Great Exhibition of 1851 "was justly ranked with the very best things of their kind, and have obtained for the producer a Prize Medal, with, in addition, a memorandum of 'special approbation'; an honour, however, which he has repudiated." From *The Crystal Palace and its Contents*, page 77. *Below:* Ornamental fire dogs by William Pierce, of Jermyn Street, London. From *The Official Catalogue* of the Great Exhibition of 1851, Vol. II, page 605.

When chimerical creatures such as the cockatrice, dragon, and gryphon replaced or accompanied representations of orthodox fauna, and florid naturalistic motifs were intertwined with formalised Rococo scrolls and shells, the results could be as confused as the ornamental fire dogs, by William Pierce, on page 139, or as untidy as the circular table below, made by George J. Morant of New Bond Street for the Duchess of Sutherland who suggested

Table and bookcase, by G. J. Morant. "The table is of elegant design, and distinguished by the finest workmanship. It was made for the Duchess of Sutherland, and, we believe, from her design. The swans are painted white, the lilies and bulrushes partly gilt and partly white. The bookcase is also white and gold, and of very pretty design." From *The Crystal Palace and its Contents*, page 160.

the design.[131] The bell made of leaves, that Wornum selected as an example of inept design, is matched by another, on the opposite page, called "The Faery Summoner," which was described as "a fanciful and pretty idea, very pleasingly realised; Puck shouts lustily, calling the spirits of the air to do his mistress's bidding."[132] Another piece of ornamental silver on the same page, an inkstand in the form of a thistle, illustrates the Victorian liking for disguise, and here the ornamental treatment has not only disguised but interfered with the function of the article. "There is a very great difference between *ornamenting* a utensil with natural objects, and *substituting* these natural objects for the utensil itself," Wornum wrote. "In the latter case, however true the details,

Ornamental silver shown at the Great Exhibition of 1851. *Above, left:* A bell described as "The Faery Summoner." (See page 140.) *Above, right:* An inkstand in the form of a thistle. It was not, ran the description, "a very happy idea, whilst the introduction of hooks or rests for the pen upon the stalk is decidedly an addition not to be found in nature; the execution, however, is highly satisfactory." *Below:* A tea and coffee service, described as "very beautiful and elaborate works; the designs, which are all punched and richly chased, representing the various stages in the culture and preparation of the tea plant. We hardly approve, however, of the taste shown in the introduction of the figures of Her Majesty and Prince Albert as ornaments or handles to the lids." From *The Crystal Palace and its Contents*, page 156.

the design is utterly false; in the former, you are in both respects true, and may be also highly suggestive and instructive. Of course, there are many natural objects which at once suggest certain uses; and we can never be wrong if we elaborate these into such implements or vessels as their own very forms or natures may have spontaneously presented to the mind. Every article of use has a certain size and character defined for it by the very use it is destined for, and this may never be disregarded by the designer; it is, in fact, the indispensable skeleton of his design, and has nothing to do with ornament. But it is upon this skeleton that the designer must bring all his ornamental knowledge to bear; and he is a poor designer if he can do nothing more than imitate a few sticks and leaves, or other natural objects wherewith to decorate it; he must give it character as well as beauty, and make it suggestive of something more than a display of sprigs and flowers gathered from the fields, or this would be mannerism indeed."(133)

Occasionally the ideas of a designer were deranged by conflicting ambitions, and the silversmith who conceived and executed the tea and coffee service shown on the lower

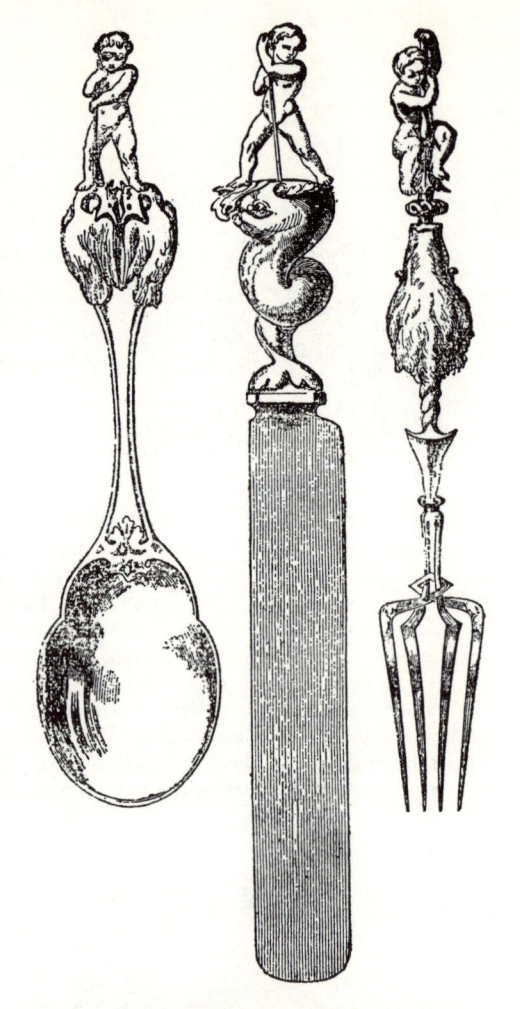

Knife, fork, and spoon, by Lambert and Rawlings. From *The Crystal Palace and its Contents*, page 297.

part of page 141 allowed naturalistic motifs to govern the form of the handles and feet, used the sides of the pots for depicting the brewing of coffee by Arabs and various stages in the culture and preparation of the tea plant, and made a loyal gesture on the lids, which were surmounted by figures of the Queen, on the tea pot, and Prince Albert, on the coffee pot. The knife, fork, and spoon on this page were described as "novel and fanciful . . . emblematic respectively of fish, flesh and fowl, three out of the 'four elements' (vegetable alone being unrepresented) of which the humblest repast and the

Above: Two silver wine flagons by Lambert & Rawlings, described as "noble in form, being after the fashion of the old camp-bottle, and decorated in the *Renaissance* style, in silver and parcel gilt. Just the sort of thing to grace the table of an old baronial hall, on a birthday or other family anniversary." *Left:* A silver claret jug, by Lias & Sons, "very handsomely shaped, ewer fashion; somewhat elastic in form, covered with vine-leaves, grapes, &c." From *The Crystal Palace and its Contents*, page 156.

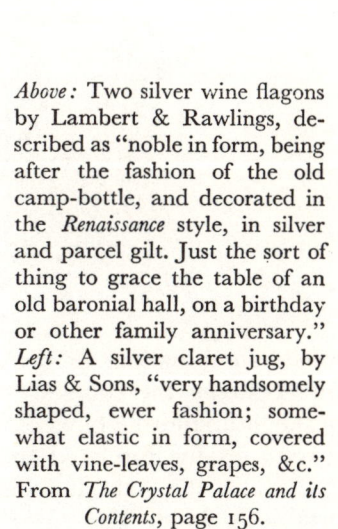

Sopwith's Monocleid Cabinet, made in black walnut. "This cabinet contains a great number of drawers and partitions, so arranged as to be especially serviceable for the keeping of various papers sorted, and the whole of them are opened by one turn of the key, there being but a single lock and a single keyhole situated externally." From *The Crystal Palace and its Contents*, page 108.

most *recherché* combinations of the *cuisine* consist. They will bear and repay inspection—between the courses."(134) No doubt the blade of the knife, the prongs of the fork, and the bowl of the spoon were adequate for their purpose, but they were totally unrelated to the handles, were in fact merely jammed into them, while the "emblematic" ornamentation must have been most uncomfortable to hold. The silver flagons and claret jug on page 143 are covered with quasi-classical decoration: the proportions of all three vessels show how designers had lost touch with the classical idiom, for acanthus leaves crawl over the bloated shapes of the flagons with the same abandon as unformalised naturalistic motifs. The black walnut cabinet on this page, with the upper panels of silvered plate glass, embellished with carved and gilded

Right: Ornamental clock by Charles Meigh & Sons, Hanley, Staffordshire. The subject is "Night and Morning," with a figure of Silence on top. From *The Official Catalogue* of the Great Exhibition of 1851, Vol. II, page 722.

Below: Black marble timepiece, "blending the Grecian and Egyptian styles." By Thomas Adams, 36 Lombard Street, London. From *The Official Catalogue*, Vol. I, page 408.

mouldings, is another example of classical motifs being used with profusion and distributed over surfaces without giving any particular emphasis to the proportions of the design: if anything, the insensitive disposition of the ornament accentuates the top-heavy effect of the upper part, and suggests that a chimney glass or overmantel is unhappily married to a sideboard. Memories of classical elegance in furniture were beginning to fade some years before the Great Exhibition; though bookcases, desks, davenports and sideboards occasionally exhibited good proportions, and some carved decoration was bold, precise and sparingly used.

Symbolic figures were as popular as naturalistic motifs, and they often com-

Gothic clock in imitation oak, by Thomas Adams, 36, Lombard Street, London. From *The Official Catalogue* of the Great Exhibition of 1851, Vol. I, page 409.

Two clocks by Edward White, of Cockspur Street, London, shown at the International Exhibition of 1862. These are typical of the ornate, massive mantelpiece clocks that were used in the dining-room and the study: more delicate designs appeared in the drawing-room, usually under a domed glass case. (Reproduced from *The Art Journal* illustrated international catalogue, 1862, page 200.)

peted for attention, as they do on the clock shown at the top of page 145, where the truncated angels flanking the dial represent "Night" and "Morning," with the figure of "Silence" above and a pair of cupids crouching below. The base consists of two recumbent dragons. The angel appeared frequently as a component in decorative compositions, or as a solitary figure making some hopeful or warning gesture, and despite their love of realism in art and of scientific explanations for everything, the Victorians never questioned the anatomical validity of the angel. Nobody ventured on any disruptive analysis

Examples of metalwork from "those inexhaustible mines of bad taste, Birmingham and Sheffield," illustrated in Pugin's *True Principles of Pointed or Christian Architecture*, pages 23 and 24.

New Sheffield pattern for a modern Castellated Grate.

Gothic-pattern wallpaper, illustrated in Pugin's *True Principles of Pointed or Christian Architecture*, and described by him as "a wretched caricature of a pointed building . . . repeated from the skirting to the cornice in glorious confusion,—door over pinnacle, and pinnacle over door. This is a great favourite with hotel and tavern keepers." (Page 25.)

Pattern of Modern Gothic Paper

of such celestial forms as Professor J. B. S. Haldane did, three-quarters of a century after the Great Exhibition, when he wrote: "An angel whose muscles developed no more power weight for weight than those of an eagle or a pigeon would require a breast projecting about four feet to house the muscles engaged in working its wings, while to economise in weight, its legs would have to be reduced to mere stilts."[135] Such a statement would have been dismissed as offensive blasphemy in the 1850's, for it was not until the end of that decade that Charles Darwin published *The Origin of Species*,[136] thus firing trains of doubt which ultimately exploded all kinds of accepted ideas, sacred, secular, and artistic.

Clock cases suffered severely from the vicissitudes of architectural taste; and monumental shapes in black marble gave sombre dignity to innumerable mantelpieces. They usually followed some variation of the classic orders, though occasionally a mixture of antique styles was attempted, of the kind shown on the lower part of page 145, where caryatids with Egyptian head-dresses support a heavy entablature with a pediment above. The assembly of Gothic odds and

Window in coloured glass, composed of national emblems. Designed by Luke Limner and made by the St. Helens Crown Glass Company. The designer has got in as much as possible without overcrowding the window with emblems, but has managed to create a general effect of confusion through a distracting intricacy of interlacing borders and bands. From *The Official Catalogue* of the Great Exhibition of 1851, Vol. II, Class 24, plate 90.

ends on page 146 was executed in imitation oak; an inchoate exercise by a designer who used scissors and paste apparently, for there is no unifying theme, and the assorted features are stuck on anywhere, while the clock-face looks like an afterthought, casually inserted. Ornate, massive clocks, incorporating architectural features, Gothic or pseudo-classic, of marble and gilded and enamelled metal, displayed their ornamental riches everywhere. Two typical examples, shown by Edward White at the International Exhibition of 1862, are reproduced on page 147.

Fifteen years before Wornum published his *Analysis of Ornament*, Pugin had described and illustrated the growing confusion of ornament with design. "It is impossible to enumerate half the absurdities of modern metal-workers," he wrote; "but all these proceed from the false notion of *disguising* instead of *beautifying* articles of utility. How many objects of ordinary use are rendered monstrous and ridiculous simply because the artist, instead of seeking the *most convenient form*, and then *decorating it*, has embodied some extravagance *to conceal the real purpose for which the article has been made!* If a clock is required, it is not unusual to cast a Roman warrior in a flying chariot, round one of the wheels of which, on close inspection, the hours may be descried; or the whole front of a cathedral church reduced to a few inches in height, with the clock-face occupying the position of a magnificent rose window. . . . But this is nothing when compared to what we see continually produced from those inexhaustible mines of bad taste, Birmingham and Sheffield: staircase turrets for inkstands, monumental crosses for light-shades, gable ends hung on handles for door-porters, and four doorways and a cluster of pillars to support a French lamp; while a pair of *pinnacles* supporting an arch is called a Gothic-pattern scraper, and a wiry compound of quatrefoils and fan tracery an abbey garden seat."[137] (See page 148.)

The sequel to such falsifications of form and function was the Venus of Milo, reproduced in miniature, in bronze or plaster, with a clock inserted in her stomach, while the logical development of the *naturalist* school of ornament was furniture made from real animals, stuffed or

The loss both of delicacy and precision in the use of classic ornament is apparent in this drawing-room chair-back from the 1836 edition of George Smith's *Cabinet-Maker and Upholsterer's Guide*. (See page 146.)

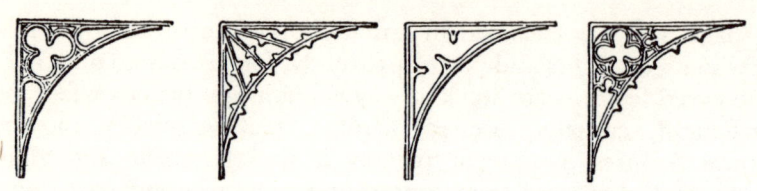

Above: Designs for cast-iron brackets to support fixed seats or tables in taverns and coffee-houses. *Below:* Eight varieties of "Gothic framing" in cast-iron for supporting independent tables.

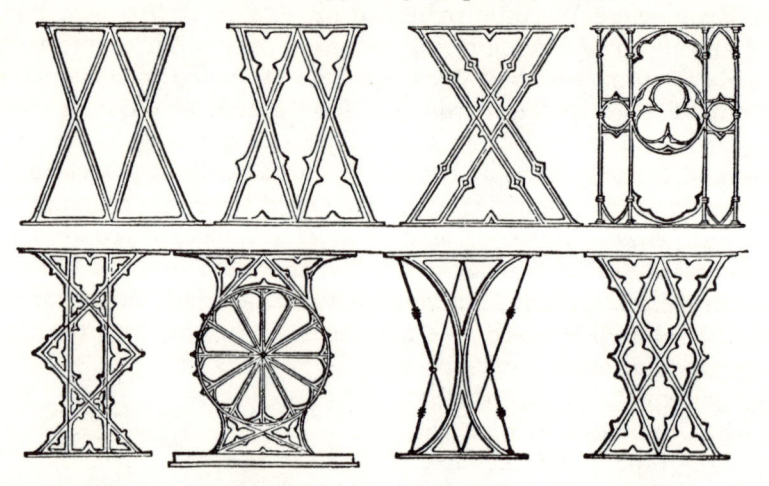

Right: Hall chair with two-piece cast-iron framework and wooden seat. *Below:* Chair frame of cast- and wrought-iron, to take a wood seat. Gothic chair, cast in three pieces and riveted together. All examples on this page are from Loudon's *Encyclopaedia* (1833). (See page 47.)

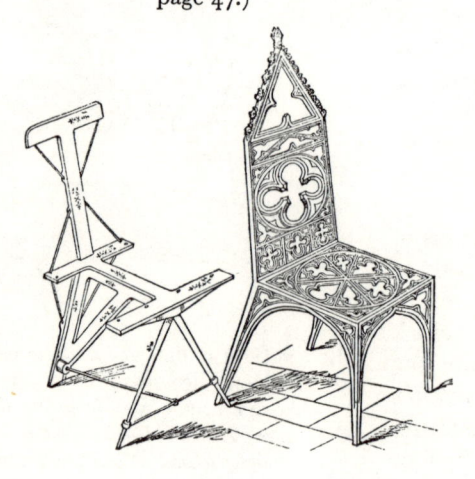

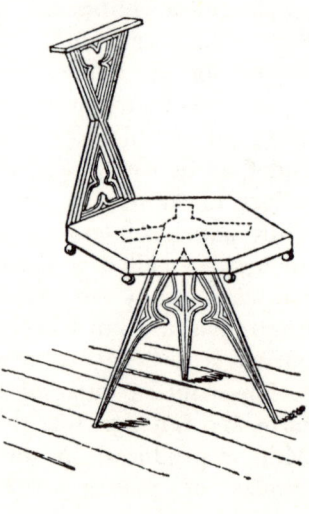

Above: A garden seat, cast at Coalbrookdale, perhaps as early as 1850. The decorative possibilities of cast-iron have been realised and exploited, unfortunately without any sense of proportion. The hoof feet are pre-Victorian survivals.

Left: A Coalbrookdale garden chair in cast-iron, a later design than the seat, and one in which firm, orderly lines give coherence to its decorative character. It may have been influenced by the work of William Morris, and the ornamental forms resemble those produced by Walter Crane and his imitators.

Drawn by Marcelle Barton and reproduced by Courtesy of the British Cast Iron Research Association.

hollowed out—a practice dating from the 1860's, when women adopted the fashion of wearing whole grouse and pheasants as hats. (When this craze was at its height, more grouse were worn than eaten; suppliers could hardly meet the demand, and received four guineas a bird.)

Early in the 70's, *The Art Journal* described, with guarded approval, the activities of Messrs. Ward and Hatchwell, naturalists of Piccadilly, who had "given a new feature to their Art—that of preserving the outward aspect and

A CATTLE-LINE CONSPIRACY.

Dufferton. Well, I could have Sworn I Hit the "Bull" that Time.
Officer in Charge (having looked through glass). No, but very Near. You've Killed the Cow in the Field to the Left!

> Metal chairs of the kind depicted in this drawing from *Judy*, August 19th, 1868, had a slender elegance of form, but such articles were not regarded as serious contributions to furnishing. They had various uses, in gardens and parks, but the fact that an original style had been developed in chair design, outside the furniture manufacturing trade—which used wood almost exclusively—escaped notice.

character of animals. The name of 'Ward,'" said the writer of the notice, "has long been honourably associated with that interesting branch of natural history, and any information comes from him with a strong claim to consideration. They have endeavoured to utilise the skins of animals and birds, and their museum contains many striking and interesting proofs that they have succeeded. Chief of them are lamps. Instead of the usual vases they introduce bird-skins, full and perfect in plumage—the owl, the eagle, the scarlet ibis, the golden pheasant, and the bird of paradise; and for hall-lamps, bears, monkeys, and leopards. There are several other adaptations, such as 'game covers' for the table; fire-screens, in which between two sheets of plate-glass humming birds are introduced; rugs of the natural fur. . . . It is difficult to convey an idea of the effect of these borrowings from nature; certainly they are very remarkable, and no doubt would startle those who sat beside them to eat or read;—we allude mainly to the lamps, though they form but one of a dozen such adaptations. Messrs. Ward have made them really refined objects of Art, not merely curious and novel and interesting."[138]

Over twenty years later, in an article on "Animal Furniture," by William G. Fitzgerald, published in *The Strand Magazine* in 1896, many examples were described and illustrated of the use of parts of animals, or whole animals, in furnishing. Since the days of ancient Egypt, and throughout the Graeco-Roman civilisation, representations of legs, wings, hooves and claws had been used in the decoration of furniture; but the Victorian desire for realism and the increasing popularity of big game hunting in various parts of the Empire encouraged the use of real animals, first in the form of mounted trophies, adapted for some practical use, and later as complete pieces of furniture. The Prince of Wales had a bear, which he had shot in Russia, stuffed and set up as a dumb waiter with a tray fixed in its front paws. Elephants' feet were hollowed out and used as liqueur stands. "One of the earliest designs was a horse's hoof—a favourite charger—made into a silver-mounted inkstand. Chairs were also made which were supported by the four legs of a rhinoceros or zebra, or a favourite horse." A baby giraffe "shot by Mr. Gardiner Muir, near the Kiboko River, in British East Africa," was made into a chair, to the design of Rowland Ward, of Piccadilly.[139] A hall-porter's chair, also modelled by Rowland Ward, was made from a young Ceylon elephant. Elephants were sometimes used as "cosy corners." Sir Edwin Landseer designed a complicated hat stand, consisting entirely of antlers. A hall clock was grasped in the jaws of a tiger; a giant argus pheasant mounted as a fire screen; arm-chairs were made from hippopotamus skulls; an ostrich leg used for a door stop; a stuffed emu supported a lamp and shade; with the whole animal, bird, and reptile world to draw on, this paying branch of taxidermy could provide plenty of variety.

"For some reason," said Fitzgerald, "innumerable monkeys were sold to light up billiard-rooms, the little animals swinging from a hoop with one hand and carrying the lamp in the other. After a time people other than those who had dead pet monkeys

Right: Occasionally a frame of flat metal strips would have an upholstered seat and back and padded arm rests, like this easy chair by Sedley of Regent Street, a London upholsterer who showed this design at the International Exhibition of 1862. (From *The Art Journal* illustrated international catalogue.)

wanted to possess these unique lamps, so that defunct simians from the Zoo had to be eagerly bought up, and Mr. Jamrach, the famous wild beast importer, was vexed with orders for *dead* monkeys. Later on less uncommon pets—parrots and cockatoos—were utilized in a similar manner, and at length this latter form of the craze reached preposterous dimensions. Will it be believed that the Bond Street house (I have it on the authority of the manager) had actually to keep a stock of *live* parrots and cockatoos, so that aristocratic customers could select one for a swinging lamp? After selection, the doomed bird was sent along to the taxidermist, killed immediately, and then mounted in the style chosen. The parrots swung in brass hoops with outspread wings, and carried the lamps on their back; whilst the cockatoos were 'chained' to a perch."(140)

As in the Georgian Age, there were periodic waves of foreign taste, which

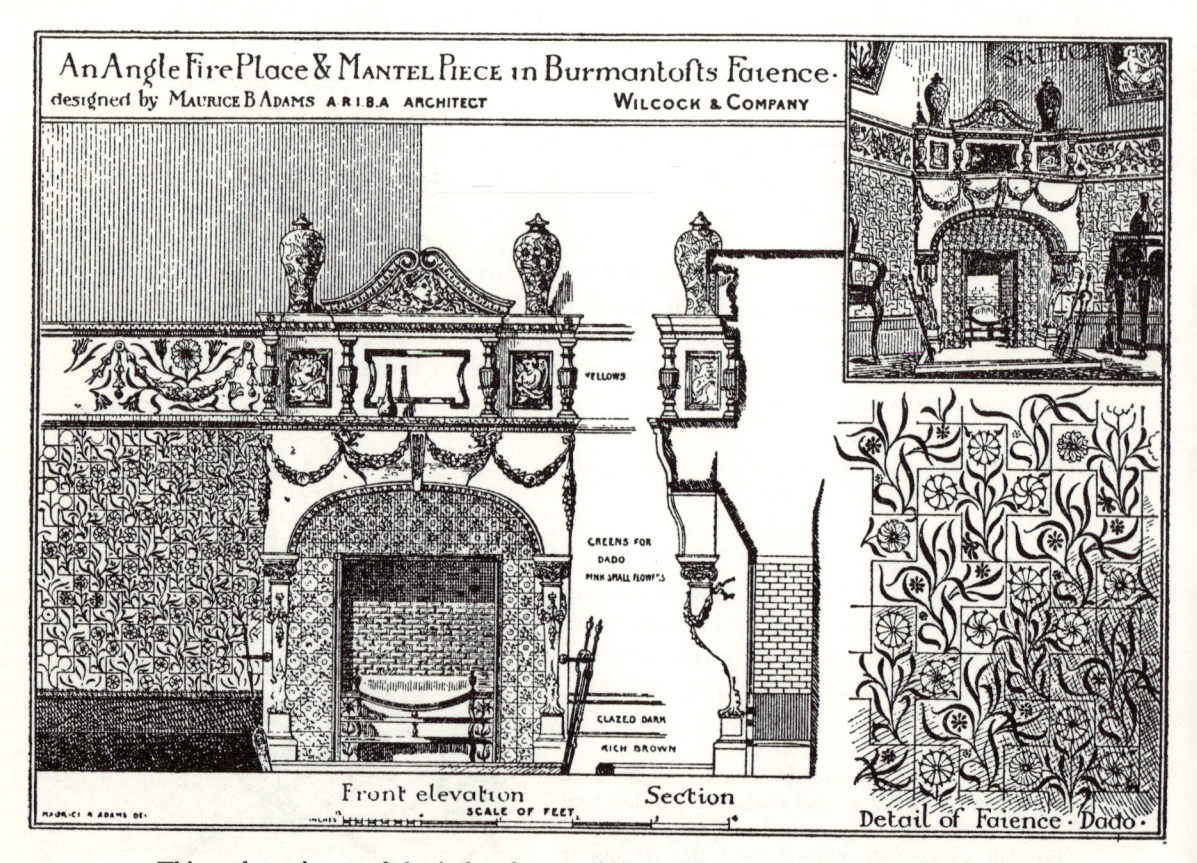

This restless mixture of classical and naturalistic motifs was commended by Robert W. Edis. The material used was "a new kind of architectural *faience*" called "Burmantofts," produced by Wilcock and Company of Leeds. From plate 1 of *Decoration and Furniture of Town Houses*.

Domestic iron and brasswork, selected by Robert W. Edis as examples of good design and illustrated on plate 20 of *Decoration and Furniture of Town Houses*. "The hanging lamp, from a design by Mr. Calcutt," he wrote, "is exceedingly graceful and common-sense in form, and, to my mind, infinitely more appropriate for a hall or staircase, than the usual telescopic fittings in general use; it can be made in wrought iron, filled in with leaded glass, for a few pounds, or even in polished brass for the price of an ordinary hall lamp." (Page 277.)

merely added to the existing confusion; for nineteenth-century designers lacked the innate sense of fitness that distinguished their Georgian predecessors; they had no sureness of touch, no feeling for style, no real certainty of what they were about. Materials as various and ductile as cast-iron and papier-mâché were temptingly available, so were innumerable mechanical processes; but they were usually dedicated to imitation and disguise. A slender and elegant style of furniture was developed in papier-mâché, inlaid with ornament of mother-of-pearl, aptly used and sparkling against the black background of chairs and small tables; and although the shapes of such chairs were often attenuated, almost spidery in effect, they were not without grace. The characteristic contemporary forms of ornament were, like the architecture the engineers created, largely disregarded. They occurred in railway buildings and equipment—on such features as the valances of station roofs and signal boxes, on the incidental decoration of locomotives and the livery of rolling stock; and a few articles were innocent of disguise, such as chairs made from metal strips, or those used in gardens and parks, which were free from the "quatrefoils and fan tracery" of the metal "abbey garden seats" that Pugin condemned.

"Nothing can be worse than art at second-hand," said Robert W. Edis, in the first of a series of Cantor lectures he delivered to the Society of Arts in 1880; "more especially when the associations and feelings of the two sets of workers, the original and the imitators, are totally different."[141] He was criticising the attempts to imitate Oriental art, which had followed a wave of taste for Indian and Japanese decoration. The criticism was equally applicable to the imitation of mediaeval ornament, which followed the handicraft revival initiated by William Morris. (See pages 96 and 99.) Nearly all the illustrations Mr. Edis used, when his lectures were published in book form in 1881, flouted the good sense of his original words; and many of them showed not only how disastrously ornament was confused with design, but how overcrowding had become identified with cosy comfort. Comfort was respectable and, like ornament, had become an end in itself, so Victorian design, like a once slim young man, became inelegantly corpulent on a rich diet of ease and profusion.

Cast-iron balconet, with classical motifs elaborately entwined above elongated scrolls. From *The Englishman's House from a Cottage to a Mansion*, by C. J. Richardson (1870). "In France," said the author, "these balconets are regarded as necessary protections at window openings. In England they are used chiefly for holding flowers."

SOURCES OF REFERENCES IN THE TEXT

CHAPTER I. THE NEW PATRONAGE AND THE DISCARDED HERITAGE

(1) *The Wrong Box*, by Robert Louis Stevenson and Lloyd Osborne. Chapter VIII.

(2) *Rides on Railways*, by Samuel Sidney. (London: William S. Orr & Company, 1851.) Pages 8–14.

(3) *The Architect in History*, by Martin S. Briggs, F.R.I.B.A. (Oxford: at the Clarendon Press, 1927.) Chapter VI, page 215.

(4) *A Short Dictionary of Furniture* by John Gloag. (London: Allen & Unwin Ltd., revised edition 1969.) Entry SPRING UPHOLSTERY, pages 236–237.

(5) *Encyclopaedia of Cottage, Farm, and Villa Architecture and Furniture*, by John Claudius Loudon. (London: Longman, Rees, Orme, Brown, Green & Longman, 1833.) Book I, Chapter III, page 336.

(6) *The Art of Conversation, with Remarks on Fashion and Address*, by Captain Orlando Sabertash. (London: G. W. Nickisson, 1842.) Chapter V, pages 181–82.

(7) *A History of Europe*, by H. A. L. Fisher. (London: Edward Arnold & Co. Complete edition in one volume, 1936.) Book II, Chapter XXIX, page 779.

(8) *Daedalus, or Science and the Future*, by J. B. S. Haldane. (London: Kegan Paul, "To-day and To-morrow series," 1924.) Page 54.

(9) *The Decline and Fall of the Roman Empire*, by Edward Gibbon. Volume I, Chapter XIII.

(10) *Lectures on Architecture and Painting*, by John Ruskin (1854). Lecture I.

CHAPTER II. ROMANTIC GOTHIC

(11) "The Gothick Taste," by J. Isaacs, M.A.(Oxon), Professor of English Language and Literature in the University of London, Queen Mary College. A lecture given at the Royal Institute of British Architects, June 17th, 1952. *Journal of the R.I.B.A.*, Volume 59, No. 9, July, 1952, page 337.

(12) *Anecdotes of Painting in England*, by Horace Walpole. (London: J. Dodsley. Third edition, 1786.) Volume IV, pages 226–27.

(13) *The Builder's Director or Bench-Mate: Being a Pocket-Treasury of the Grecian, Roman, and Gothic Orders*, by Batty Langley. (London: H. Piers, 1751.)

(14) *A Description of Fonthill Abbey and Demesne*, by John Rutter. (Shaftesbury: printed and published by J. Rutter, 1822. Third edition.) Section II, pages 27–28.

(15) *Ibid.*, Section II, page 21.

(16) *The Seven Lamps of Architecture*, by John Ruskin. Preface to the second edition.

(17) *Household Furniture and Interior Decoration, Executed from Designs*, by Thomas Hope. (London: Longman, Hurst, Rees & Orme, 1807.)

(18) *John Nash*, by Sir John Summerson. (London: George Allen & Unwin Ltd., 1935.) Chapter IX, page 160.

(19) *An Attempt to Discriminate the Styles of Architecture in England, from the Conquest to the Reformation*, by Thomas Rickman. (London: Longman, Rees, Orme, Green & Longman. Fourth edition, 1835.) "English Architecture," pages 38–39.

(20) *A Biographical Dictionary of English Architects, 1660–1840*, by H. M. Colvin. (London: John Murray, 1954.) Entry THOMAS RICKMAN, pages 498–99.

(21) *Architecture: Nineteenth and Twentieth Centuries*, by Henry-Russell Hitchcock. (The Pelican History of Art. Penguin Books Ltd., 1958.) Chapter VI, pages 117–18.

(22) *The Stranger in Liverpool.* (Liverpool: Printed and Sold by T. Kaye. Ninth edition, 1829.) Page 142.

(23) Colvin, *op. cit.*, page 499.

(24) *The Creative Centuries*, by Henry John Randall. (London: Longmans, Green & Co., 1944.) Chapter 9, page 61.

CHAPTER III.   CHRISTIAN GOTHIC

(25) *Hammersmith: A Study in Town History*, by Warwick H. Draper. (Hammersmith: James Chamerlen, 1913.) Section III, pages 16–18.

(26) *John Nash*, by Sir John Summerson. (London: George Allen & Unwin Ltd., 1935.) Chapter II, page 47.

(27) Summerson, *op. cit.*, page 47.

(28) *Recollections of A. N. Welby Pugin and his Father, Augustus Pugin*, by Benjamin Ferrey, F.R.I.B.A. (London: Edward Stanford, 1861.) Chapter II, page 16.

(29) Ferrey, *op. cit.*, page 17.

(30) Ferrey, *op. cit.*, page 17.

(31) Ferrey, *op. cit.*, Chapter III, page 35.

(32) *Pugin, a Mediaeval Victorian*, by Michael Trappes-Lomax. (London: Sheed & Ward, 1933.)

(33) *Contrasts: or a parallel between the Noble Edifices of the Middle Ages, and Corresponding Buildings of the Present Day, shewing the Present Decay of Taste*, by A. Welby Pugin, Architect. (London: Charles Dolman. Second edition, 1841.)

SOURCES OF REFERENCES IN THE TEXT

(34) Trappes-Lomax, *op. cit.*, Chapter VII, page 75.
(35) *2000 Years of England*, by John Gloag. (London: Cassell & Company Ltd., 1952.) Chapter XIX, page 263.
(36) Gloag, *op. cit.*, Chapter XIX, pages 263–70.
(37) Pugin, *Contrasts*, Chapter II, page 16.
(38) Pugin, *op. cit.*, Chapter II, pages 17–18.
(39) *A History of the Protestant "Reformation" in England and Ireland*, by William Cobbett. (London: Charles Clement, 1824.) Letter V, paragraph 155. The pages of the book are not numbered.
(40) Cobbett, *op. cit.*, Letter XVI, paragraph 478.
(41) Cobbett, *op. cit.*, Letter II, paragraph 37.
(42) Cobbett, *op. cit.*, Letter VI, paragraphs 181–82.
(43) Cobbett, *op. cit.*, Letter V, paragraph 155.
(44) Cobbett, *op. cit.*, Letter VI, paragraph 183.
(45) Cobbett, *op. cit.*, Letter VI, paragraph 183.
(46) Pugin, *Contrasts*, "Conclusion," page 51.
(47) *Talleyrand*, by Duff Cooper. (London: Jonathan Cape. Academy Books edition, 1934.) Chapter III, page 80.
(48) Duff Cooper, *op. cit.*, Chapter III, page 80.
(49) *Cottage Economy*, by William Cobbett. (London: C. Clement, 1822.) Introduction, pages 2–3.
(50) *Eminent Victorians*, by Lytton Strachey. (London: Chatto & Windus. 1921 edition.) "Dr. Arnold," page 191.
(51) Cobbett, *Cottage Economy*, page 10.
(52) *Rugby*, by C. R. Evers. (London: Blackie & Son Ltd., 1939.) Chapter III, page 36.
(53) *Peter Simple*, by Frederick Marryat. The remark is made by O'Brien. Chapter LI.
(54) Pugin, *Contrasts*, Chapter I, page 7.
(55) *The True Principles of Pointed or Christian Architecture*, set forth in Two Lectures delivered at St. Marie's, Oscott, by A. Welby Pugin. (London: John Weale, 1841.) Lecture I, page 1.
(56) *An Apology for the Revival of Christian Architecture*, by A. Welby Pugin. (London: John Weale, 1843.) Pages 1–2.
(57) Pugin, *op. cit.*, page 4.
(58) Pugin, *op. cit.*, page 5.
(59) Pugin, *op. cit.*, pages 7–9.
(60) Ferrey, *op. cit.*, Chapter XVIII, page 248.
(61) Trappes-Lomax, *op. cit.*, Chapter IX, page 85.

(62) Ferrey, *op. cit.*, Chapter XVIII, page 244.

(63) Ferrey, *op. cit.*, Chapter XVIII, page 246.

(64) Ferrey, *op. cit.*, Chapter XIII, pages 164–66.

(65) "Religious Art," by John T. Emmett. Reprinted from *The British Quarterly Review*, October 1st, 1875, and included in *Six Essays*, published by Unwin Brothers, London, 1891.

CHAPTER IV. LOUDON AND DOWNING

(66) Letter to William Tait, Esq., from J. C. Loudon, dated Bayswater, February 29th, 1832. New York Public Library, MS. Division. Miscellaneous Papers.

(67) *Observations on Laying out Farms in the Scotch Style adapted to England*, by J. C. Loudon. (London: John Harding, 36 St. James's Street, 1812.)

(68) *Self-Instruction for Young Gardeners*, by the late J. C. Loudon. (London: Longman, Brown, Green & Longmans, 1847.) Preface to memoir on the life of the author by his widow, Jane Loudon.

(69) Discussion following Miss Violet Markham's paper, "Joseph Paxton and his Buildings," given at the Royal Society of Arts, November 15th, 1950.

(70) *The Mummy! A Tale of the Twenty Second Century*. Three volumes. (London: Henry Colburn, 1827.)

(71) *The Suburban Gardener, and Villa Companion*, by J. C. Loudon. (London: Longman, Orme, Brown, Green & Longmans, 1838.) Chapter III, page 136.

(72) *The True Principles of Pointed or Christian Architecture*, by A. Welby Pugin, page 58.

(73) *Encyclopaedia of Cottage, Farm, and Villa Architecture and Furniture*, by J. C. Loudon. (London: Longman, 1833.) Design XX, page 919.

(74) *Encyclopaedia of Cottage, Farm, and Villa Architecture and Furniture*, edited by Mrs. Loudon. (New edition, 1846, with Supplement.) Pages 1145–47.

(75) *Op. cit.*, page 1147.

(76) *Our Iron Roads*, by Frederick S. Williams. (London: Ingram, Cooke & Co., 1852.) Chapter X, page 236.

(77) *Cottage Residences; or a Series of Designs for Rural Cottages and Cottage Villas, and their Gardens adapted to North America*, by A. J. Downing. (New York and London: Wiley & Putnam. Second edition, 1844.) Page 25.

(78) *Cottage Residences*, by A. J. Downing, page 33.

(79) *The Sketch Book of Geoffrey Crayon, Gent*. [Washington Irving.] (London: John Murray. New edition, 1824.) Volume II, "Christmas Eve," pages 35–36. The book was dedicated to Sir Walter Scott.

(80) *Cottage Residences*, by A. J. Downing, page 137.

(81) *Op. cit.*, page 149.

SOURCES OF REFERENCES IN THE TEXT

(82) *Op. cit.*, page 150.

(83) *Op. cit.*, page 99.

(84) *The Architecture of Country Houses*, by A. J. Downing. (New York: D. Appleton & Co., 1850.) Section I, pages 37–38.

(85) *Specimens of Ancient Furniture, Drawn from Existing Authorities*, by Henry Shaw, F.S.A., with Descriptions by Sir Samuel Rush Meyrick, K.H., LL.D., F.S.A. (London, William Pickering, 1836.)

(86) *Furniture with Candelabra and Interior Decoration*, designed by R. Bridgens. (London: William Pickering, 1838.)

(87) *A Walk from London to Fulham*, by Thomas Crofton Croker, F.S.A., M.R.I.A. Revised and edited by his son, T. F. Dillon Croker, F.S.A., F.R.G.S. (London: William Tegg, 1860.)

(88) *Op. cit.*, Chapter VII, pages 212–15.

(89) *Op. cit.*, Chapter VII, page 229.

(90) "The Seeing Eye," by Sir Francis Meynell, R.D.I. Paper delivered before the Royal Society of Arts, October 25th, 1954. *Journal of the Royal Society of Arts*, Volume CIII, No. 4939, page 9.

(91) *The Seven Lamps of Architecture*, by John Ruskin. First published in 1849. Preface to the second edition.

CHAPTER V. RUSKIN AND MORRIS

(92) *The Tragedy of John Ruskin*, by Amabel Williams-Ellis. (London: Jonathan Cape, 1928.) Chapter III, page 30.

(93) *The Institution of the Christian Religion*, by John Calvin. Translated by Thomas Norton. (London: Printed by Anne Griffin for Joyce Norton and R. Whitaker, 1634.) Book I, Chapter II, page 12.

(94) *The Art Journal*, Volume 13, page 5 (1874). "John Ruskin, the Art-Seer," by J. J. Jarves.

(95) *The Tragedy of John Ruskin*, by Amabel Williams-Ellis. Part III, Chapter XVII, pages 182–83.

(96) *Op. cit.*, page 184.

(97) *The Life of William Morris*, by J. W. Mackail. (London: Longmans, Green & Co., 1899.) Volume I, Chapter II, pages 46–47.

(98) *Op. cit.*, Volume I, Chapter I, page 15.

(99) *Tom Brown's Schooldays*, by Thomas Hughes. (First published, 1857.) Chapter VI.

(100) Mackail, *op. cit.*, Volume I, Chapter I, page 16.

(101) *Stalky & Co.*, by Rudyard Kipling. (London: Macmillan & Co., 1899.)

(102) *How I Became a Socialist*, by William Morris. Originally published in *Justice*, June 16th, 1894.

(103) Mackail, *op. cit.*, Volume I, Chapter IX, page 283.

(104) *A Factory as it might be*, first published in *Justice*, 1884 (No. 18).

(105) *Useful Work versus Useless Toil*, first published in 1885 as a pamphlet by the Socialist League.

(106) The opening lines of *The Wanderers*, the Prologue to *The Earthly Paradise*, first published in 1868.

(107) *Pioneers of Modern Design, from William Morris to Walter Gropius*, by Nikolaus Pevsner. (The Museum of Modern Art, New York. Second edition, 1949. The original edition was issued in 1936.) Section I, page 10.

(108) Several of the passages between pages 93 and 95 are condensed from Chapter VIII of my book, *Men and Buildings*. (Chantry Publications Limited. Second revised and illustrated edition, 1950.)

(109) *Useful Work versus Useless Toil* (1885).

(110) *News from Nowhere*, by William Morris. Chapter III.

(111) *Gothic Architecture*, an address by William Morris to the Arts and Crafts Exhibition Society, 1889. Printed at the Kelmscott Press in 1893.

(112) *Ibid.*

(113) *The Architect in History*, by Martin S. Briggs, F.R.I.B.A. (Oxford: Clarendon Press, 1927.) Section VIII, page 368.

(114) Pevsner, *op. cit.*, Section I, page 9.

CHAPTER VI. THE CLASSIC TRADITION AND THE UNRECOGNISED STYLE

(115) *The Art Journal* (1868), Volume VII, pages 224–25.

(116) *McKim, Mead & White*, by C. H. Reilly. (London: Ernest Benn Ltd., 1924.) Page 23.

(117) *Designs for Factory, Furnace and other Tall Chimneys*, by Robert Rawlinson. (1862. No publisher's name appears on the title page, and the work was apparently privately printed for the author.)

(118) *Our Iron Roads*, by Frederick S. Williams. (London: Ingram, Cooke & Co., 1852.) Chapter VII, page 153.

(119) *Ibid.*, Chapter VII, page 154.

(120) *British Railway History, 1830–1876*, by Hamilton Ellis. (London: George Allen & Unwin Ltd., 1954.) "Notes on Plates," page 421.

(121) *The Life of George Stephenson and of his son Robert Stephenson*, by Samuel Smiles. (London: John Murray. 1868 edition.) Part II, Chapter XVIII, page 477.

(122) *Works in Iron*, by Ewing Matheson, M.Inst.C.E. (London: E. & F. N. Spon. Second edition, 1877.) Page 227.

SOURCES OF REFERENCES IN THE TEXT 165

(123) *The Crystal Palace and its Contents: An Illustrated Cyclopaedia of the Great Exhibition of the Industry of All Nations, 1851*. (London: W. M. Clark, 1852.) Pages 88–89.

(124) *Cast Iron in Building*, by Richard Sheppard, F.R.I.B.A. (London: George Allen & Unwin Ltd., 1945.) Section 5, page 63.

(125) *Isambard Kingdom Brunel*, by L. T. C. Rolt. (London: Longmans, Green & Co., 1957.) Chapter 12, pages 231–32. The letter quoted is dated January 13th, 1851.

CHAPTER VII. ORNAMENT AND DESIGN

(126) *Analysis of Ornament*, by Ralph N. Wornum. (London: Chapman & Hall. Sixth edition, 1879, is quoted.) Chapter I, pages 4–5.

(127) *Ibid.*, Chapter II, pages 8–9.

(128) *Sunny Memories of Foreign Lands*, by Harriet Beecher Stowe. (London: Sampson Low, Son & Co., 1854.) Letter II, page 15.

(129) Wornum, *op. cit.*, Chapter II, page 9.

(130) Wornum, *op. cit.*, Chapter II, page 10.

(131) *The Official Catalogue* of the Great Exhibition, 1851. Volume II, page 745.

(132) *The Crystal Palace and its Contents*, page 156.

(133) Wornum, *op. cit.*, Chapter II, pages 10–11.

(134) *The Crystal Palace and its Contents*, page 297.

(135) *Possible Worlds*, by J. B. S. Haldane. (London: Chatto & Windus, 1927.) "On Being the Right Size," pages 22–23.

(136) The full title was: *On the Origin of Species by Means of Natural Selection, or the Preservation of Favoured Races in the Struggle for Life*. The book appeared on November 24th, 1859.

(137) *The True Principles of Pointed or Christian Architecture*, by A. Welby Pugin. (London: John Weale, 1841.) Lecture I, pages 23–24.

(138) *The Art Journal*, Volume XI, December, 1872. "Minor Topics of the Month," page 314.

(139) "Animal Furniture," by William G. Fitzgerald. *The Strand Magazine*, September, 1896. Volume XII, pages 273–74.

(140) *Ibid.*, page 275.

(141) *Decoration and Furniture of Town Houses*, by Robert W. Edis, F.S.A., F.R.I.B.A. (London: Kegan Paul & Co., 1881.) Lecture I, page 9.

THE PLATES

The frontispiece illustrates the basic difference between the Victorian and Georgian periods; it was a spiritual difference exposed by architecture, and the contrast between the buildings expressing the impassioned, striving beliefs of Pugin and the happy urbanity of Wren's work is so marked that the lives of those two men might have been separated by four hundred years instead of eighty-nine. The great Georgian architects and designers worked in the classic idiom; some of them flirted with Gothic, a harmless enough flirtation when conducted by gifted amateur designers like Sanderson Miller and men of taste like Horace Walpole; but the charming antiquarian exercises in Gothic that amused the modish world of the eighteenth century became romantic and got out of hand early in the nineteenth. This phase is illustrated in plates 1 and 2. The fashion faded out; innocent fantasies were ousted by the moving moral earnestness of the Gothic Revival which inspired vastly different structures from Strawberry Hill, Eaton Hall, and Fonthill Abbey. Plate 3 shows where morally earnest design ended.

Some of the notable men who wrote and built and exercised an influence on taste and design through their work appear on plates 4 and 5: there were many others, but the six whose portraits are included made a powerful impact on their contemporaries and helped to change the environment of life, often with perplexing results. Some architectural components of that environment are illustrated on plates 6 to 12. Classic architecture survived, often without vitality, though sometimes achieving such splendour as the Greek Doric portico at Euston and the portal of the Box Tunnel on plate 13.

The railways provided a new form of patronage for architecture, and some of the railway engineers, like Brunel, created a new structural technique which represented a fresh movement in architecture, characteristic of the period, but unrecognised as such at the time and despised by the cheer-leaders of the Gothic Revival. Some of the new forms evolved by engineers and such gifted architects as Decimus Burton, who used materials like glass and iron in imaginative association, are shown on plates 14 to 19. An authentic Victorian style of decoration arose, continuing in contemporary materials an old English tradition of design, and examples of this in cast iron are given on plates 20 and 21. Other forms of decoration appear on plates 22 and 23, and the last plate, 24, shows our grimmest inheritance from the Victorian age—the industrial scene.

Plate 1. TWO INTERIORS AT EATON HALL, CHESHIRE

Built for Lord Grosvenor by William Porden (1755–1822), between 1804 and 1812, Eaton Hall was in the Strawberry Hill and Fonthill Abbey tradition of fashionable Gothic, when it was still regarded as a modish and charming style, and not as a visible expression of moral earnestness. Porden had been a pupil of James Wyatt, the designer of Fonthill. The house was remodelled by Alfred Waterhouse, after 1867, though some of Porden's interiors were preserved. Reproduced from *Views of Eaton Hall*, by J. C. Buckler, 1826. (See page 83.)

Right: The Saloon.

Below: The Drawing-room.

Plate 2. GOTHIC IN THE GEORGIAN TRADITION: FANTASTIC, ROMANTIC, AND MUCH TOO GENTLEMANLY TO BE EARNEST

Above: The south-west view of Fonthill Abbey, Wiltshire, designed by James Wyatt for William Beckford, and built 1796–1807. (From the frontispiece of John Rutter's *Description of Fonthill*, third edition, 1822.) *Right:* The Scott Memorial in Prince's Street Gardens, Edinburgh, designed by George Meikle Kemp, and inaugurated in 1846. One of the last large scale examples of Romantic Gothic in the Georgian tradition. *Photograph by Tom Scott, Edinburgh.* *Below:* St. Luke's Church, Liverpool, designed by John Foster, and erected 1811–31. This orderly, rather prosaic building lacks the "splendid confusion" of Romantic Gothic, nor has it any of the fiery earnestness of the Gothic revivalists. (See page 11.) *From a contemporary print in the author's possession.*

Plate 3. THE APOTHEOSIS OF THE GOTHIC REVIVAL

Above, left: The Albert Memorial in Kensington Gardens, designed by Sir George Gilbert Scott, and erected 1863–72. (*Photograph by Richard C. Grierson, A.R.I.B.A.*) The design was anticipated by Thomas Worthington some fifteen months before Scott had created his idea of the memorial, and the first published design for it appeared in *The Builder*, September 27th, 1862. *See above, right.* (See "The Battlefield: A Pictorial Review of Victorian Manchester," by Cecil Stewart. *Journal of the R.I.B.A.*, May, 1960, page 240.) Worthington's design was erected in Albert Square, Manchester.

Plate 4. WRITERS WHO INFLUENCED VICTORIAN TASTE AND THE VICTORIAN SCENE

Right: John Ruskin (1819–1900), whose books and lectures exerted a profound influence on architects and designers and their patrons. He wrote and spoke with passionate sincerity; the whims and prejudices of his personal taste were accepted as eternal principles by those who acknowledged his authority, and his denigration of classical architecture helped to destroy the last traces of Renaissance inspiration in England. *Reproduced by courtesy of the Trustees of the National Portrait Gallery.*

Left: John Claudius Loudon (1783–1843), landscape gardener, architect, author, and compiler of encyclopaedias. He published Ruskin's first article, for he had the gift of recognising genius and the opportunity for encouraging young men of talent. (See page 45.) His *Encyclopaedia of Cottage, Farm, and Villa Architecture and Furniture,* first issued in 1833, gave a pre-view of Victorian taste. *From an oil painting by John Linnell, dated 1840–41, in the possession of the Linnean Society of London, by whose courtesy it is reproduced.*

Plate 5. MEN WHOSE WORK INFLUENCED VICTORIAN TASTE AND THE VICTORIAN SCENE

Above, left: Robert Stephenson (1803–59), civil engineer. From the engraving in *The Life of George Stephenson and his son Robert Stephenson,* by Samuel Smiles.

Above, right: Augustus Welby Northmore Pugin (1812–52), ardent champion of the Gothic Revival. *From a portrait in the possession of the Royal Institute of British Architects.*

Above, left: Sir George Gilbert Scott (1811–78), the most prolific architect of the Gothic Revival. *From the painting by George Richmond, R.A., at the Royal Institute of British Architects.*

Above, right: William Morris (1834–96), poet, craftsman, and instigator of the handicraft revival. *Reproduced by courtesy of the Trustees of the National Portrait Gallery.*

Plate 6. EXAMPLES OF LOUDON'S ARCHITECTURAL WORK

Left: Wood Hall Farm, Pinner, Middlesex. This was a seventeenth-century farmhouse, reconstructed by Loudon, 1809–10, after he had acquired the property. It marked the beginning of his architectural practice, and provided a model for the small rural or suburban villa which was copied with variations for three-quarters of a century.

Right: The double detached suburban villa in Porchester Terrace, Bayswater, built by Loudon in 1837–38, which became his residence and office. It was the prototype of innumerable suburban houses, in London and other cities, and preserved some traces of the classical tradition. (See page 40 and plate 18.)

Photographs by Sidney Newbery.

Left: Suburban development, with semi-detached houses, showing the influence of Loudon's *Encyclopaedia*. Part of the west side of Vardens Road, Battersea, built between 1860 and 1868. *From a drawing by David Owen.* (See page 92 for east side development of this road.)

Plate 7. *Above:* St. Saviour's Vicarage, Coalpitheath, Gloucestershire, designed by William Butterfield to go with his first church and built 1844–45. *Below:* The Red House, at Upton, Kent, built by Philip Webb for William Morris, 1859–60. *Both illustrations reproduced by courtesy of The National Buildings Record.* (See page 94.)

Plate 8. Right: Paddington Station Hotel, designed by Philip Charles Hardwick (1822–92) and built early in the 1850's; it was then the largest and most luxurious hotel in England. The design was deeply influenced by contemporary French taste. *From plate 41, Cassell's Old and New London. Below:* The Garrick Club in Garrick Street, designed and built in 1864 specially for the Club by Frederick Marrable, superintending architect to the Metropolitan Board of Works. *Reduced from the architect's drawing of the façade, in the possession of the Garrick Club, and reproduced by courtesy of the Committee.*

Plate 9. Above: The Langham Hotel, designed by John Giles and built 1864–66, a bold but rather overwhelming landmark in mid-Victorian London. *From plate 45, Cassell's Old and New London. Below:* New Scotland Yard, Victoria Embankment, designed by Norman Shaw and built 1887–90. *Reproduced by courtesy of The National Buildings Record.*

Plate 10. The Natural History Museum, in Cromwell Road, South Kensington, designed by Alfred Waterhouse (1830–1905), and built 1873–81. It is a Victorian version of Romanesque architecture, faced with terracotta slabs and embellished with zoological subjects, which adorn the façade. Like the Imperial Institute shown opposite, it is an unhappy example of the bankruptcy of architectural inspiration in the second half of the nineteenth century, when dead styles and oddments of decoration were transferred from sketch books to drawing-boards, after the Gothic Revival had ceased to attract converts, and architects browsed aimlessly in the past.
Photographs by Richard C. Grierson, A.R.I.B.A.

Plate 11. The Imperial Institute, South Kensington, designed by Thomas Edward Colcutt (1840–1924), and built 1887–93. (See page 104.) *Photograph by Richard C. Grierson, A.R.I.B.A.*

Plate 12. Air view, looking north, of the site between Cromwell Road and Kensington Gardens. *Photograph by Aerofilms Limited.* This site, bought out of the proceeds of the Great Exhibition of 1851, was used for buildings dedicated to scientific and artistic education. In the foreground, the Natural History Museum extends its frontage along Cromwell Road (see plate 10), in the centre the Imperial Institute stands (see plate 11), with the Albert Hall at the north of the site, and the Albert Memorial beyond in Kensington Gardens. In 1851, when the Crystal Palace was on its original site in Hyde Park, there were gardens and nursery grounds south of Kensington Gore, but these were enclosed by the buildings of this concentrated cultural centre. How admirably it was planned may be seen from this view.

Plate 13. *Above:* The Greek Doric portico of Euston Station, the terminus of the London and North Western Railway, designed by Philip Hardwick, 1835–37. *Below:* The classic portal of the Box Tunnel on the Great Western Railway, designed by Isambard Kingdom Brunel, towering above the double broad gauge track like some Roman triumphal arch. From a drawing by J. C. Bourne. *Both subjects reproduced by courtesy of British Railways.*

Plate 14. *Above:* The General Railway Station, Chester, designed by Francis Thompson in collaboration with Robert Stephenson, 1844–48. From a lithograph of a water-colour drawing, dated 1860. *Crown Copyright Reserved. Below:* Arrival of the Christmas train at Shoreditch Station on the Eastern Counties Railway, designed by Sancton Wood, 1848–49. From *The Illustrated London News*, December 21st, 1850.

Plate 15. *Above:* Interior of Temple Mead Great Western Railway Station, Bristol, designed by I. K. Brunel, and built 1839–40. *Below:* Interior of the shed, Lime Street Station, Liverpool. This replaced an earlier station, and was enlarged in this form, 1846–51, by Richard Turner, a contracting engineer who designed and executed the shed which was 360 feet long with a span of 153½ feet. A further enlargement was made in 1867, to the design of William Baker, Chief Engineer of the London and North Western Railway, and Francis Stevenson, the Assistant Engineer. When this work was completed, Lime Street Station was the largest in the world. *Both subjects reproduced by courtesy of British Railways.*

Plate 16.
CONCESSIONS TO
TRADITION IN
BRIDGE BUILDING
AND THE RISE OF
A NEW STYLE

Above: Clifton Suspension Bridge, designed and begun by Isambard Kingdom Brunel, and completed by W. H. Barlow. (See plate 17.) *Reproduced by courtesy of the National Buildings Record.*

Right: Brooklyn Bridge, New York, which spans the East River. Designed by John A. Roebling in 1867, and opened to traffic, May 24th, 1883. *From a pictorial souvenir of New York, published about 1880. In the author's possession.*

Plate 17. Hungerford suspension bridge, looking towards the north bank of the Thames. Designed by Isambard Kingdom Brunel, and opened on May 1st, 1845. Originally known as Charing Cross Bridge, it had a short life, and was removed in 1860; the chains and ironwork were sold and re-used for the suspension bridge that crosses the Avon at Clifton, near Bristol. (See plate 16.) The two brick piers of the suspension towers were retained, and they bear the bridge that now carries the railway from Charing Cross Station across the river. The Hungerford suspension bridge was the first to be erected in the Metropolitan area in the Victorian period. (See illustrations of Albert and Hammersmith bridges on pages 120 and 121.) *From a contemporary coloured print in the author's possession.* A far lighter and more elegant structure by the same designer was the Saltash Bridge, shown below, which carried the Great Western Railway across the Tamar. It was opened by the Prince Consort in 1859. *Photograph reproduced by courtesy of The Times.*

Photograph copyright "Country Life"

Plate. 18. The Great Conservatory at Chatsworth, built during 1836–40, and demolished in 1920. In 1956 some fresh facts came to light which suggested that although Paxton originated the idea of the great glass house, the architect for the complete edifice, and all the structural details, was probably Decimus Burton. The documentary evidence that Burton was the designer is set forth in an article entitled, "Who was the Architect of the Great Conservatory at Chatsworth?" by Francis Thompson, C.B.E., F.S.A., Director of the Devonshire Collections, published in *Derbyshire Countryside*, Vol. 21, No. 5, August–September, 1956, pages 12–13.

Right: Curvilinear glazing on a conservatory dome, designed by Loudon for his house in Porchester Terrace, Bayswater. (See plate 6, also pages 40, 42, and 43.)
Photograph by Sidney Newbery.

Plate 19. *Left:* The Palm House, Kew Gardens, Surrey, 1845–47. Designed by Decimus Burton and Richard Turner. This is a development on a much greater scale of Loudon's curvilinear glazing technique. (See plate 18, also pages 40, 42, and 43.) *Reproduced by courtesy of Sir John Summerson.*

The New York Crystal Palace, built in 1853 to house the World's Fair, and destroyed by fire in 1856. There was nothing adventurous about this building: it was "an inferior copy of the London structure." (*New York City Guide*, 1939, page 218.) Compare this with Paxton's design on pages 130 and 131. *From a contemporary engraving in the author's possession.*

Both photographs copyright "Country Life"

Plate 20. Interior decoration in the Coal Exchange, Lower Thames Street, London, built in 1847–49, by the City Architect, James Bunning. (The exterior is shown on page 102.) *Above, left:* One of the encaustic paintings of coal miners in the galleries, by Frederick Sang. *Above, right:* Detail of cast-iron decorative features on the ground floor, with emphasis on the cable motif.

Right: Base of cast-iron lamp standard, outside St. George's Hall, Liverpool. *Photograph by the author.*

Plate 21. *Right:* Cast-iron balcony and stairway balustrades on house at Parkgate, Wirral, Cheshire, which retain the lightness and elegance of Georgian design. *Photograph by the author.*

Below: Decorative cast-iron work on the gates of the Sailors' Home, Liverpool. This medley of motifs is a tribute to the ability of the ironfounder, not to the skill of the designer. *Reproduced by courtesy of The National Buildings Record.*

Plate 22. An unremarked contemporary style arose in railway and industrial architecture, which continued an old English tradition of design, authentic and robust. The valance on the platform roof of Battle Station, Sussex, is an example of this style, which had nothing false about it, like the mock-Gothic windows above the platform roof. *Reproduced by courtesy of British Railways.* An equally distinctive, but more elaborately contrived style, was created by William Morris, of which the detail from the Armoury at St. James's Palace, shown below, is an example. 1866–67. *Reproduced by courtesy of the Warburg Institute.*

Plate 23. Detail from the Throne in the House of Lords, designed by A. W. N. Pugin, *circa* 1846. Pugin alone of the Gothic revivalists could give such vitality to the opulent decoration of a long-dead style: he was an interpreter of the spirit of mediaeval design, not a diligent and uninspired copyist like so many of his contemporaries. *Reproduced by permission of The Ministry of Works: Crown Copyright Reserved.*

Plate 24. The industrial scene was set in Victorian times, and it still endures in hundreds of districts in England, Scotland and Wales. From the painting, "A Street in the Valley," by Donald Matthews, an artist born in the Rhondda Valley. *In the possession of Richard Thomas & Baldwin Ltd., by whose courtesy it is reproduced.*

INDEX

Figures in italics apply to references in captions

Abbotsford, Roxburghshire, 12
Adams, Thomas, *145*, *146*
Adventures of Mr Verdant Green, The, 7
Aird, John, *108*
Aird, Sir John, Bart., *108*
Aire Bridge, Leeds, *117*, 118
Albert, Prince Consort, *103*, 104, 106
Albert Bridge, London, 118, *120*
Albert Hall, London, 105, *105*, 106
All Saints, Margaret Street, London, *70*
Analysis of Ornament, 136, *138*, 151
Anderson, James, *124*
Animal furniture, 151, 153-6
Antique furniture, 62 et seq.
Apology for the Revival of Christian Architecture, An, 34
Arboretum Britannicum, 40
Architectural Magazine, The, 45
Architecture of Country Houses, The, 62, 66, 67
Armchairs, 4, 5, 7
Arnold, Dr Thomas, 20, 32, 88
Art Journal, The, 84, *96*, *99*, 101, *109*, *147*, *153*, *155*
Arts and Crafts Exhibition Society, 93
Atkinson, William, 12
Attempt to Discriminate the Styles of Architecture in England, An, 14, 15

Baker, Sir Benjamin, 123, *124*
Baker, William, *122*, 123
Balconet, *158*
Banbury, Oxon., *127*
Banks, Sir Joseph, 41
Barlow, W. H., *81*
Barnsley, Sidney, *94*
Barry, Sir Charles, 35, 36, 37
Barry, E. M., *37*, 85
Bartlett, William A., *75*

Bath and Bristol and the Counties of Somerset and Gloucester, *14*
Battersea, London, 103
Battle of the Styles, 3, 8, 14, 38, 97, 101, 135
Bazalgette, Sir Joseph, 116, *119*, *120*, *121*
Beckford, William, 11
Bede, Cuthbert, *see* Bradley
Beehives, *8*
Bell, J., 128
Belloc, Hilaire, 28
Biedermier style, 137
Birmingham Gazette, *126*
Blake, William, quoted, 32
Blore, Edward, 12
Box Tunnel, 110
Bradley, Edward, 7
Bretton Hall, Yorks., *43*
Brewer, Richard, *80*, 86
Bridgens, Richard, 62
Bridges, 116 et seq.
Bridges, *120*
Brighton, Pavilion, 13
Britannia Bridge, Menai Strait, *119*, 122, *123*
British Cast Iron Research Association, *153*
British Quarterly Magazine, *91*
Britton, John, *14*, 20
Brooks, James, 87
"Brotherhood, The," 90. See also Pre-Raphaelites.
Brown, Ford Madox, 95
Browne, Hablôt Knight (Phiz), *13*
Brunel, Isambard Kingdom, 110, *110*, *114*, 116, 119, 123, 128, 130, 135
Brunel, Isambard Kingdom, quoted, 130
Buck, Nathaniel and Samuel, 10
Builder, The, 77
Builder's Director or Bench-Mate, The, 11
Buildings of England: London, *18*, *106*
Bunning, James Bunstone, *102*

"Burmantofts," *156*
Burne-Jones, Sir Edward, 90, 95
Burton, Decimus, 41, *42*, 133
Busby, C. A., 12
Butterfield, William, 70

Cabinet-Maker and Upholsterer's Guide, *151*
Calvin, John, 74
Cambridge, Eastern Counties Railway Station, *114*
Campden Hill, London, 107, *108*
Capes, A. and J. M., 70, 73, 74, 76, 87
Capitol, Washington, U.S.A., 59
Carew, Peter, *133*
Carlton House Terrace, London, 16
Cast Iron in Building, *126*, 128
Cast iron, 16, *45*, 47, 116, *117*, 118, 123, *126*, 127, *127*, 128 et seq., *152*, 153, *158*
Castle of Otranto, The, 10
Chairs, drawing-room, *151*
Chairs, hall, *152*
Chairs, kitchen, *45*
Chairs, metal, *154*, *155*
Charing Cross Bridge, London, 116
Chatsworth, Derbyshire, 41, *42*, 133
Chelsea Bridge, London, 118, *118*, *119*
Chesterton, Gilbert Keith, 28, 110
Chichester Cross, 22, *24*
Christchurch, Herne Bay, *33*
Clark, William Tierney, 116, *121*
Clifton Suspension Bridge, 116
Clocks, ornamental, *145*–7, *149*, *150*, *151*
Coal Exchange, London, *102*
Coalbrookdale Bridge, Shropshire, 116, *117*
Coalbrookdale Company, *117*, *129*
Cobbett, William, 6, 28 et seq.
Cobbett, William, quoted 28–30
Cockerell, Sir Charles, 13, 34
Cockerell, Samuel Pepys, 13, *14*
Coke, Thomas William, Earl of Leicester, 29
Colcutt, Thomas Edward, 104
Collier and Plucknett, Warwick, *99*
Columbia Market, Hackney, London, *89*
Colvin, H. M., quoted 16
Combat and Carnival, *133*
Commonweal, The, 93
Comparative View of the Common and Curvilinear Modes of Roofing Hothouses, A, 41
Congleton Viaduct, Staffs., *110*

Contrasts, 6, 22–8, *23*, *24*, *26*–*8*, 30, 34
Cooper, A. Duff (Lord Norwich), 31
Cottage Residences, 59, 62, *63*–5
Cottages, *50*, 51, *52*–5, 57, *58*, 62, *63*–5
Cottingham, L. N., *127*
Cragg, John, 16
Crane, Walter, *153*
Croker, Crofton, 66
Croker, Dillon, 66
Cromwell, Oliver, quoted, 28
Crystal Palace, London, 41, 79, *125*, *131*, 132, *132*, 133, *133*
Crystal Palace and its Contents, The, 128, *129*, *132*, *133*, *139*–*44*
Crystal Way, *115*
Cubitt, Thomas, *103*, 104
Cumberland Gate, London, *127*
Currey, Henry, 104, *104*

Daedalus, 5
Dance, George, the younger, 10
Darbishire, Henry Astley, *89*
Darby, Abraham, 116
Darwin, Sir Charles, 149
Decoration and Furniture of Town Houses, 94, 156, 157
Designs for Factory, Furnace and other Tall Chimneys, 107, *109*
Devonshire, Duke of, 133
Dickens, Charles, 1, 6, *13*, 23
Discourse of Forest Trees and the Propagation of Timber, 29
Downing, Andrew Jackson, 39, 59, 61, 62, 63–7, 69, *69*
Downing, Andrew Jackson, quoted, 61, 62

Eastnor Castle, Herefordshire, 12
Easy chairs, 4, *5*, *7*
Eaton Hall, Cheshire, 11, *17*, 82, *83*
Edis, Robert W., 94, 156, 157, 158
Edis, Robert W., quoted, 157, 158
Egyptian Hall, Piccadilly, London, 13
Egyptian ornament, 13
Electric-telegraph instruments, 2, *3*
Elements of Architecture, The, 8
Ellis, Hamilton, quoted, 112
Emmett, John T., 80, 91
Emmett, John T., quoted, 38, *91*, 10
Encyclopaedia of Agriculture, 40

INDEX

Encyclopaedia of Cottage, Farm, and Villa Architecture and Furniture, 16, 34, 39, *43,* 44, *45–8, 47,* 49, *50,* 51, *52–9,* 62, 104, *152*
Encyclopaedia of Gardening, 40
Encyclopaedia of Plants, 40
Encyclopaedia of Trees and Shrubs, 40
Engineers, 3, 106 et seq.
Engineering, 124
Englishman's House from a Cottage to a Mansion, The, 158
Euston Station, London, 3, 128
Evelyn, John, 29
Evelyn, John, quoted, 8, 9
Examples of Gothic Architecture, 20
Executive Mansion, Washington, U.S.A., 59

Fastnet Rock Lighthouse, 47
Faulkner, 95
Ferrey, Benjamin, quoted, 20, 21, *31,* 38
Fisher, H. A. L., quoted, 5
Fitzgerald, William G., 155
Fitzgerald, William G., quoted, 155, 156
Fliegende Blätter, 137
Fonthill Abbey, Wilts., 11
Foreign Office, London, 101
Forsyth, James, *92, 110*
Forth Bridge, Scotland, 123, *124, 125*
Fowke, Captain Francis, 105, *105,* 106, 107
Fowler, Sir John, 123, *124*
Fox, Sir Charles, *132, 133*
Fox, Henderson & Co., *132, 133*
Fraser, Alexander, *108,* 110
Fraser's Magazine, 66
Furniture with Candelabra, 62

Garden seats, *153*
Gardener's Magazine, 43, 44
Gardening for Ladies, 39
Garrick Club, London, 105
Gascoyne, Somers T., *80*
Gibbon, Edward, 4, 8
Gibbon, Edward, quoted, 9
Gimson, Ernest, *94*
Glass, 130, 132 et seq., 150
Glasshouses, 41, *42,* 43
Glazing, 41, 133
Gothic remains, 10 et seq.
Gothic Revival, 19 et seq., 72 et seq., 98, *125*
Gothic Revival in U.S.A., 56, 59

Gough, Hugh Roumieu, *18*
Grace Church, New York, 59
Grand Junction Water Works Company, 107, 108
Graphic, The, 83
Gray, Euphemia (Mrs. John Ruskin), 71
Great Exhibition, of 1851, 128, *129, 130,* 132, *133,* 136, *139, 141,* 146, 149
Great Victorian Way, 115, 134
Great Western Railway, 110, *110*
Greek Revival, 102
Guide to Western Architecture, 124, 125
Guildhall, London, 10
Gwrych Castle, Denbighshire, 12

Haldane, J. B. S., quoted 5, 6, 149
Hammersmith Bridge, London, 116, 118, *119, 121*
Hammersmith Parish Church, London, *18,* 19
Handicraft Revival, 31, 93–5, 158
Hawkins, Rhode, *82*
Heal, Sir Ambrose, *94*
History and Antiquities of the Parish of Wimbledon, 75
History of the Protestant Reformation, A, 6, 28, 30
Hogarth, William, 22
Hope, Thomas, 13
Horticultural Society, 41
House of Commons, report of, 115, 134
Houses of Parliament, London, 35, 36, *37,* 38
Hungerford Bridge, *see* Charing Cross Bridge
Huxley Building, London, *107*

Illustrated London News, The, 114, 118
Imperial Institute, London, 104
Indian ornament, 13
Industrial Revolution, 6, 132
Inns, 47
International Exhibition, 1862, *92, 147,* 151, 155
International Exhibition, 1872, *96, 99*
Ipswich Tunnel, 112
Irving, Washington, 28, 61

Jones, Sir Horace, *134*
Jones, Inigo, 8
Judy, 154

King's Cross, Battlebridge, London, 23, 25
Kipling, Rudyard, 1, 90
Knight, H. C., *135*

Labels, decorative, 1, *2*
Lamb, Edward Buckton, *59*
Lancaster, Osbert, 22
Landseer, Sir Edwin, 155
Langley, Batty, 11
Law Courts, London, 38, *85*, 97
Leather, John and George, *117*, 118
Leaves from the Journal of Our Life in the Highlands, *103*
Lectures on Architecture and Painting, 75, 78
Lemercier, Jacques, 3
Lethaby, William Richard, quoted, 49
Letter-boxes, *127*, 128
Lichfield, Earl of, 112, *113*
Life of William Morris, 18
Lime Street Station, Liverpool, 128
Limner, Luke, *150*
Literary Journal, 42
Liverpool, Prince's Landing Stage, *126*, 128
London and North Western Railway, *122*, 123
London County Council, *120*
Loudon, Mrs Jane, 39, 41, 44, 45
Loudon, John Claudius, 16, 34, 39 et seq., 69, 78, 104, *152*
Loudon, John Claudius, quoted, 50, 51
Lounging, 4, 7
Luscombe, Devonshire, 12

Macdonald, Henry, 90
Mackail, J. W., *18*
Mackail, J. W., quoted, 88
Mackenzie, Sir George, 41
Magazine of Natural History, 45
Maidenhead Bridge, Berks., *110*
Mallet, John, 47
Mallet, Robert, 45, 47
Manchester School, 32
Manchester Ship Canal, *122*
Markham, Miss Violet, 42
Marlborough College, Wilts., 88
Marrable, Frederick, 105
Marryat, Frederick, quoted, 32
Matheson Ewing, quoted, *125*, *127*, *128*
McKim, Mead and White, 102, 103

Mechanophilus, 135
Meigh, Charles & Sons, *145*
Metropolitan Board of Works, 105, 120
Meynell, Sir Francis, quoted, 69
Meyrick, Sir Samuel Rush, 62
Millais, Sir John, 71
Modern Painters, 72
Modern Style of Cabinet Work, The, 5, 7
Moffatt, W. B., *74*, *75*
Monocleid cabinet, *144*
Moorish ornament, 13
Morant, George J., 140, *140*
Morris, William, *18*, 28, 88 et seq., *153*, 158
Morris, William, quoted, 90, 91, 93, 95, 97
Morris and Company, *94*, 95
Moseley, William, *115*
Muir, Gardiner, 155
Municipal Corporation Act, 1835, 23

Napoleon of Notting Hill, The, 110
Nash, John, 12, 16, 20, 128
National Gallery, London, 136
New Scotland Yard, London, *92*
Newburgh, U.S.A., 69
News from Nowhere, 91, 95

Official Catalogue of the Great Exhibition, *3*, *8*, *117*, *131*, *133*, *139*, *145*, *146*, *150*
Old and New Churches of London, The, 70, 73, 74, 76, 87
Old and New London, 25, *81*, *89*, *102*, *106*, *107*, *130*, *134*
Ordish, Rowland Mason, *120*
Origin of Species, The, 149
Ornament, 1, 13, 136 et seq.
Osborne House, I.O.W., *103*, 104
Östberg, Ragnar, 100
Our Iron Roads, 1, *51*, *56*, *110*, *111*, *111*, *112*, *112*, *113*, *122*
Oxford Museum, Oxford, 86

Paddington Station, London, *114*, 128
Page, Thomas, *118*, *119*
Paine, Tom, 116
Palazzo Farnese, Rome, 8
Palm House, Kew Gardens, London, *42*, 133
Palmerston, Henry John Temple, 3rd Viscount, 81, 97, 101

INDEX

Panorama of Science and Art, 14
Papier-mâché, 157
Parochial Institutions, 43
Pavilion, Brighton, 13
Paxton, Sir Joseph, 41, 42, 132, *132*, 133, *133*, 134
Paxton and the Bachelor Duke, 42
Peel, Sir Robert, 23
Personal and Professional Recollections, 74, 81, 85
Pevsner, Dr Nikolaus, *106*
Pevsner, Dr Nikolaus, quoted, *18*, 93, 100
Phiz, see Browne
Pickwick Papers, The, 13
Pierce, William, *139*, 140
Pillar-boxes, 127. See also letter-boxes
Police force, 23
Pollio, Marcus Vitruvius, 8
Porchester Terrace, Bayswater, London, *40*, *41*, *42*
Porden, William, 11, 13, *17*, *83*
Potts, William, 138, *139*
Praeterita, 71
Pratt, Samuel, 4
Pre-Raphaelites, 72. See also "Brotherhood"
Price, Cormell, 90
Price, Sir Uvedale, 12, 29
Price, Sir Uvedale, quoted, 11
Pritchard, Thomas Farnolls, 116, *117*
Pryor's Bank, The, Fulham, London, 66, 68
Public houses, *46*, *47*
Pugin, Augustus Charles de, 20
Pugin, A. W. N., 6, 12, 20 et seq., 61, 72, 100, *148*, 158
Pugin, A. W. N., quoted, *17*, 23–7, 32, 34–6, 49, 50, *53*, *80*, 151
Pugin: a Mediaeval Victorian, 21
Pulpits, *91*
Putney, London, 103

Quarterly Review, *104*
Queen Anne Revival, 102

Railway architecture, 51, 110 et seq.
Randall, Henry John, quoted, 16
Rastrick, John, 116, 118
Rawlinson, Sir Robert, 107, *108*, *109*
Recollections, Ferrey's, 21, 31
Recollections of Richmond, *80*
Red House, Upton, Kent, 94, 95, 98

Regent Street, London, 16
Reid, William, 2, *3*
Reilly, Sir Charles, quoted, 103
Remarks on the Construction of Hothouses, 41
Renwick, James, 59
Ricauti, T. J., *56*
Richardson, C. J., quoted, *158*
Richmond, Surrey, Fire Brigade Station, *80*, *86*
Rickman, Thomas, 14, 16, 128
Rickman, Thomas, quoted, 15
Rights of Man, The, 116
Robertson, John, 45
Robinson, Peter Frederick, 13, 16, 57, 60
Romantic Movement, 10 et seq.
Roofs, glazed curvilinear, *41*, *42*
Roslin Chapel, Scotland, *12*
Rossetti, Dante Gabriel, 95
Royal Albert Bridge, Saltash, 119, 123
Royal Society, 41
Royal Victoria Patriotic School, Wandsworth Common, London, *82*
Rugby School, 88
Runcorn railway bridge, 122, *122*, *123*
Rural Architecture, 57, 60
Ruskin, Euphemia, 71
Ruskin, John, 6, 28, *33*, *38*, 45, 47, 49, 71 et seq., 90, *92*, *94*, *97*, 100, 136
Ruskin, John, quoted, 9, 12, 72, 73, 75, 78, 79, 81, 82, 104, 105, 130, 132
Ruskin, Margaret, 71
Russell, Sir Gordon, *94*
Rutter, John, 11

St. Anne's, Soho, London, *26*, *27*
St. Columba's, Shoreditch, London, *87*
St. George's, Liverpool, 16
St. Giles's, Camberwell, London, 74
St. Helens Crown Glass Company, *150*
St. James-the-Less, Westminster, London, 73
St. John's, Leeds, 19
St. Marie's Grange, nr. Salisbury, *31*
St. Mark's, Battersea, London, *86*
St. Mary Abbots, Kensington, 76
St. Mary-le-Park, Albert Bridge Road, London, *86*
St. Mary's, Wimbledon, 75
St. Matthias, Richmond, Surrey, 76, 77
St. Michael's, Huyton, Lancs., 19, *21*
St. Michael's, Liverpool, 16

St. Pancras Hotel, London, 81, 97
St. Pancras Station, London, *80, 81*
St. Paul's Cathedral, London, 97
St. Paul's, Hammersmith, London, *18*
St. Philip's, Liverpool, 16
St. Thomas's Hospital, London, 104, *104*
Saracenic ornament, 13
Scott, Sir George Gilbert, 68, 75–7, 80, 81, 85, 97
Scott, Sir George Gilbert, quoted, *15, 74, 81*
Scott, Major-General Henry Young Darracott, 105, *105, 106, 107*
Scott, Sir Walter, 1, 10, *12*, 79
Seddon, John Pollard, *18*
Semper, Gottfried, *106*
Seven Lamps of Architecture, The, 72, 130
Sezincote House, Glos., 13, *14*
Shaw, Henry, 62
Shaw, Norman, *92, 99*, 102
Sheppard, Richard, *126*
Sheppard, Richard, quoted, 128
Shugborough Park Tunnel, 112, *113*
Sidney, Samuel, quoted, 3
Silver, ornamental, 140, *141*, 142, *142, 143*
Six Essays, *80, 91*
Sketch Book, The, 61
Sketches of Curvilinear Hothouses, 41, *42*
Smiles, Samuel, quoted, 119
Smirke, Sir Robert, 12
Smith and Founders' Director, The, *127*
Smith, George, *151*
Smithfield, London, Metropolitan Meat Market, *134*
Smithsonian Institute, Washington, U.S.A., 59
Socialist League, 93
Society for the Protection of Ancient Buildings, 68
Society of Arts, 158
South Kensington, London, 104
Specimens of Ancient Furniture, 62
Specimens of Gothic Architecture, 20
Spirit of the Public Journals, The, 12
Springs, in upholstery, 4
Staunton Harold, Lincs., church at, 19
Steel, 123
Stephenson, George, *135*
Stephenson, Robert, 119, *123*, 135
Stevenson, Francis, *122*, 123
Stevenson, Robert Louis, quoted, 1, *12*
Stockholm, Town Hall, 100

Stones of Venice, The, 72
Story of the Stephensons, Father and Son, *135*
Stowe, Harriet Beecher, quoted, 137
Strand Magazine, The, 155
Strawberry Hill, Twickenham, Middlesex, 10, *15*
Street furniture, *127*
Street, George Edmund, 73, *85*, 90, 97
Suburban Gardener and Villa Companion, The, *40, 41, 49, 56, 57, 60*
Summerson, Sir John, quoted, 20
Sutherland, Duchess of, 140, *140*
Swiss Cottage, St. John's Wood, London, 13
Sylva, 29

Talleyrand-Périgord, Charles Maurice de, 31
Taylor, Rev. Fitzwilliam, quoted, *133*
Telford, Thomas, 116, 118
Tennyson, Alfred Lord, quoted, 6, 135
Tew Park, Oxon., 40
Thackeray, William Makepeace, 1
The Mummy!, 44
Thornbury, Walter, 25, *102*
Thornbury, Walter, quoted, *134*
Tipton, Staffs., No. 1 Lock, *126*
Tower Bridge, London, 123, *125*
Tragedy of John Ruskin, The, 86
Trappes-Lomax, Michael, 21
Trappes-Lomax, Michael, quoted, 22
Treatise on the Theory and Practice of Landscape Gardening, 69
Trinity Church, New York, 59
True Principles of Pointed or Christian Architecture, The, 17, 32, *33*, 49, 53, *80*, 148, *149*
Turner, Richard, *42*, 133

Union Debating Rooms, Oxford, 86
United Services College, Westward Ho, 90
Upholstery, use of springs in, 4
Upjohn, Richard, 59

Vardens Road, Battersea, London, *92*, 104
Victoria, Queen, *103*
Victoria and Albert Museum, London, *106*
Villas, *48*, 50, 51, *52*, 65
Vitruvius, *see* Pollio

INDEX

Walford, Edward, *81, 89*
Walford, Edward, quoted, *89, 106, 107, 130*
Walk from London to Fulham, A, 66
Wallpaper, *149*
Walpole, Sir Horace, 4th Earl of Orford, 10, 11, *15*, 67
Ward, Rowland, 155
Ward and Hatchwell, 153–5
Warton, Thomas, 29
Waterhouse, Alfred, *82, 83, 85*
Watts, George Frederick, *73*
Wear Bridge, Sunderland, 116
Webb, Miss Jane (Mrs. Loudon), 44
Webb, Philip, 94, *94*, 95, 98
Wells, H. G., 1
Wells, William, *57*
Westcheap conduit, London, *26, 27*
Whistler, James McNeill, 38
White, Edward, *147*, 151
White, William, *86*

Wilcox and Company, Leeds, *156*
Williams, Frederick S., 1, *110*, 111, *112*
Williams, Frederick S., quoted, 51, *56*, 111, 112, *113*, 122
Williams-Ellis, Mrs. Amabel, 86
Williams-Ellis, Mrs. Amabel, quoted, 86, 88
Wilson, E. J., 20
Woburn, Beds., 51, *56*
Wood Hall Farm, Pinner, Middlesex, 40
Wood, Sancton, *114*
Woodward, Benjamin, 86
Wornum, Ralph Nicholson, 136, 137, *138*, 140, 151
Wornum, Ralph Nicholson, quoted, 136–8, 140, 142
Wotton, Sir Henry, 8
Wren, Sir Christopher, 97
Wrought iron, 123, 132
Wyatt, James, 11
Wyatt, Matthew Digby, *114*, 128, 130
Wye Bridge, Chepstow, 118